WHATEVER YOU ARE

DON'T!

Jerusalem, Athens and Rome
I'd see them before I die,
But I'd rather not see any one of the three
Than be exiled forever from Skye.

Sheriff Nicholson

WHATEVER YOU ARE DOING...
DON'T!

THE ADVENTUROUS LIFE OF

RUARAIDH HILLEARY

Skirinish publishing

This edition is first published by
Skirinish Publishing
Skirinish Cottage
Skeabost Bridge
Isle of Skye
Scotand
IV51 9PF

www.skirinishpublishing.com

ISBN Hardback: 9780995488205
ISBN Paperback: 9780995488212

British Library Cataloguing-in-Publication Data
A catalogue record for this book is available from the British Library.

Typeset: Eugene Rijn R. Saratorio
Cover design: Marta Wawrzyniak-Chade
Cover illustration: David Shaw Stewart
Cartoons by 'Loon' are © Alasdair Hilleary

In loving memory of my darling daughter Iona.

Contents

Acknowledgments

I should start this tale by thanking my son Duncan and nephew Alec Shaw Stewart for hiring a reporter friend to spend a week with me while she recorded all this rubbish! They set out to do this as a record for our family, but once it had been transcribed, we decided it might actually work best in the form of a book.

So then I must thank Caroline Macdonald for her incredible tolerance of my writing changes as she knocked it all into some sort of readable sequence. So here goes.

CHAPTER ONE

Childhood in Skye

Those balmy pre-war days in Skye were the most formative of my childhood, with relations all over the island's main Estates of Greshornish, Edinbane, Skeabost, Orbost, Lyndale, Kingsburgh and Tote as well as the many crofts in the south end of Skye at Breakish, Kyle Farm and Waterloo.

As I was the eldest grandson on both sides of my family no thoughts of class ever struck me, although high standards were the norm, and I regret now that the native Gaelic was somehow being replaced by English, and losing a certain connection in the process.

We drove to Skye in the Bentley pretty well every school holiday, navigating the old roads, some still with grass in the centre, that twisted through the Highlands evoking memories of the romantic names such as Tomdoun, Ballachuilish and Dornie Ferry, as the scenery merged into the wild. The Bentley was a huge blue and black sedanca de ville 8 Litre GN 1896 with a plaque on the dashboard with the chassis, engine numbers and the weight, which was 2 tons 15 hundredweight.

When I was young we usually stayed with my Mother's parents Duncan and Ishbel MacLeod at Skeabost, a grand but welcoming 14 bedroom Victorian mansion at the head of Loch Snizort, but sometimes at The Lodge in Edinbane with my Father's parents Teddy and Edith Hilleary. The former had been born on a croft in the south end of Skye while the latter's family had been Tacksmen in Skye for 500 years or more.

There were always a wonderful mixture of guests in both houses and I particularly remember Harry Lauder, the comedian and singer, Elsa Schiaparelli, an Italian fashion designer who invented culottes, and Rev George MacLeod, founder of the Christian Iona Community. Any one of them could be found in the kitchen having a cup of tea with the baker, who was also a relation of course.

As a boy, I spent much of my time in the gun room with the Skeabost keeper, Jock Urquhart. He became my close friend and I spent the happiest and most wonderful days with him on the hill.

Urquhart (as my grandfather called him) taught me so many things. I have especially vivid memories of him in the gun room, in his tweed suit and black brogues, usually with a rod in his hand. The brown lino on the floor and the Hardy rod rack outside promised future excitements on the river or the grouse moor. The mahogany gun cupboard hid the guns and rifles behind locked glass doors. There were salmon flies galore and the whole room reeked of gun oil and the hill. That smell created a lifetime fascination in my mind.

There seemed to be nothing that Jock did not know about the wild. He set the scene for me always to wonder at nature and its sheer scale.

With Jock I got to know every burn and detail of the Kinloch hill; coming back from a stalk along the path that leads beside the shore through the birch woods, he would be carrying the fore-end of a stag and me with the haunches over my shoulders, dripping with blood; exhausted and exhilarated as we made for home.

The 8 Litre Bentley at Skeabost with my father and me 1937

Jock was with me for my very first day after a stag, when I was about 12 years old. We had arranged to meet Fraser, the resident stalker on Lord Macdonald's deer forest at Sconser, early one September morning. We set out along the old Sconser road, stopping to spy as we climbed the hill. It was a typical Skye day: the early morning mist had cleared and the sun threw shadows in between the showers. When a shower came it obscured the hill, but when it cleared, even for a few moments, we had a good view. I had never been stalking before and so was full of excitement and apprehension.

As we reached a point close to where the road started to flatten out, we saw four stags in Corrie na Laogh on Ben Dearg. They were in a spot accessible from below, if we crawled up the burn.

Fraser knew the hill backwards. Dressed in tweeds, a deerstalker, and with a moustache, he was older than Urquhart and chose to stay below while Urquhart and I started the stalk. Fraser probably thought I was too young, or that maybe I would make too much noise, so he just sat and waited at the bottom of the hill.

Up the burn we crept and a perfect hump appeared just where we wanted it, on which to rest the rifle. Urquhart looked round at me and beckoned me up beside him, and there were the stags. Two were lying down, the largest one was standing, square on. I had a clear shot at his heart.

Down he went but the others, startled but unclear about the direction from which the shot had come, stood up and waited. "Go on" said Urquhart, "take the next fellow," so I shot him too. The other two were much smaller, knobbers actually, and they started up the scree that led out of the corrie to the left.

They were not making good progress and stopped to look round at their fallen friends, so I shot number three. I remember thinking, this is rather too many, a bit excessive, but the blood was up and the killer instinct was taking over. Jock was encouraging me: I do not think I would have done it otherwise. The last beast turned to try another direction off the scree to the right, and he failed too, so I regret to say that Urquhart, who was very excited by this time, said "Go on, have the last one as well." I am not really proud of that massacre now, but at the time it was extremely exciting.

At home that night, exhausted after pulling the stags as far as we were able, covered in blood - for Urquhart had fairly sploshed my face in it - nobody would believe that I had shot four stags on my very first day out.

The police called later, to ask if I had had a licence, for the word had got out about my slaughter. A dram seemed to do the trick for no more was heard from that direction. I have always passed that spot, on what is now the main Sconser road over the hill, with memories of that day, vivid as ever. It set the pattern for my love of the chase after a stag that still lingers today.

Jock's stories inspired my love of stalking. I hope I have passed that on to others. I have since been the stalker for eight young men to get their first stag over the years, including my brother Alasdair, my son Duncan, Charles and Andrew Macdonald, Hugh and Alan Macdonald and Patrick Shaw Stewart. Every one was a thrill, but particularly when it was for my grandson Archie.

***

I was born at Craigarn Hall, Bridge of Allan, on February 8th 1926. My father, Iain, was working in the Whisky trade for Grandfather (Duncan MacLeod) at the time. Craigarn Hall was the factor's house on the Keir estate, family home of David Stirling, founder of the SAS.

My father was the eldest of three sons. He was a tall, good-looking man of 6'2", and a great athlete at his school, Repton, before going up to Trinity College, Cambridge.

His Father, known as Teddy, was Major Edward Langdale Hilleary OBE. (Military), TD. DL. Serbian Order of the White Eagle and Legion d'honneur (2). Teddy and his brother Roland, (Uncle Ro), had been cut off by their father, a lawyer, for going into "trade" when they started the White Heather Laundry in London. But they ended up being awarded Royal Appointments and their laundry became extremely successful with uniformed drivers who all had leather leggings and were very smart.

Teddy had joined The Lovat Scouts in the First World War and been Adjutant to Colonel Kenny Macdonald DSO of Tote, in North Skye.

My Mother, Rubie, was Duncan MacLeod's eldest daughter. She had been sent off to boarding school in England and finishing school in Paris. Her father, who was born in a croft house and schooled at what is now the Red Skye Restaurant in Breakish, had gone out into the big wide world, leaving Skye first for Liverpool and then to America to sell lemonade, but discovered that there was a better future in the whisky business with which he made a fortune, much of which probably came from Prohibition.

He returned to Skye and bought the Skeabost Estate, from my father's side of the family.

My parents were married at St Giles Cathedral, in Edinburgh in 1924. It must have seemed a magic marriage of the two Skye families, for they were the eldest sibling of each. I suspect that they were pretty spoiled by both families, as there was plenty of money on each side. This meant that my father never really had to try very hard at anything.

His job in the whisky trade for his father-in-law did not last long. He was then bought a Directorship in Mono Containers, a factory at Willesden, North West London, making paper cups. My father remained at that company, as a director, for more than ten years, until the start of the war in 1939 when they rented various properties in the south starting with 44 Lowndes Street, London, then Boveney Court, near Eton; Sandford Manor, Waltham St. Lawrence; and then Woodlands Park, Great Missenden, just before the Second World War.

When the war started my father left Mono Containers and tried to join the Scots Guards and then the RAF. But he was turned down by both. At 36 he was just the wrong age. He eventually joined the United Kingdom Commercial Corporation (UKCC), an organisation formed by Jack Hambro for the government in 1940 as a cover for their real work, which was buying strategic goods before the enemy could get them. It was significant war work, but it did open me to some unkind remarks from certain boys at school whose parents were in uniform.

I remember little else about this time, nor of the many house moves we made as a family, but I have been told one story about our time in London, when I was still in a pram. I was being wheeled across the road towards the park in my pram by the nursery maid, Cathy MacFarlane with my brother Alasdair in another pram being wheeled by "Nanno", the nanny who came to us when I was born. Apparently a passing taxi hooked the spring of my pram onto the rear bumper of his vehicle, and I was whisked off down Kensington High Street. I have no recollection of this adventure but possibly that did spark an early interest in tobogganing...or something of the sort.

***

Although much of my early childhood was spent in the south, I can always remember being proud of the fact that Skye was my background. I felt very sorry for people who had to come from England. They could not possibly have had as much fun as we did.

At Skeabost there were several steps in the passage leading up to the kitchen and the great challenge was to ride a bike up the steps and try and get round the kitchen table before Mrs Buchanan, the very fierce cook, could get you with a rolling pin. She got very crabby when we did this, so we had to be quick.

Then there was lovely Bella, the housekeeper who used to encourage us to get into trouble and loved all the mischief. She would feed me sugar lumps out of the huge metal bin in the storeroom and I remember her as being very old but she was probably only in her fifties. She was a great ally, and friend who would love to tell a slightly doubtful story.

My Grandmother was a lovely homely and welcoming person who in-variably seemed to run the house without any effort; although we did test her tolerance at times that would evoke the "whatever you are doing, don't" response, when riotous behavior had gone too far; and after a while, my grandfather would threaten the cousins with "if you go on behaving like that you will turn out like the Hilleary boys".

So in 1936 my parents bought Tayinloan Lodge, an old coaching inn that had been the shooting Lodge for the Lyndale Estate. Lyndale, originally a Macdonald Elizabethan house with a Victorian extension, added by Lord Napier, surrounded by wonderful woods. It belonged to my Father's brother, Uncle Rocky and his wife, Aunt Gay.

Tayinloan Lodge

Tayinloan was not far from the shore at Clachamish, between Dunvegan and Portree. My mother started a garden there which my father later extended and developed to the extent that it was open to the public with many special rhododendrons, a Mexican flame tree and a wide variety of shrubs, all pretty well now gone wild.

I lived there with my mother and younger brothers, Alasdair and Ewan, and with Catherine Nicoll, known to everyone as Nanno. Nanno came to the family when I was born and stayed with us until she died. She was a big feature in my life, perhaps more of a mother than my mother sometimes. She always referred to us as "her Boys" and would have died for us I'm sure.

Chrissie Campbell, a lovely matronly figure from an old Skye family who was devoted to us all, was mistress of the kitchen. She was a great friend and lived across the glen, in a croft at Suledale. Chrissie was married to Duncan Campbell, the postman. There was also a series of other young girls who helped in the house.

Hector Munro, who had been in the Camerons in the First World War and with the Gurkhas, which he called "the Gurks", looked after the garden and the boat. Hector and Mrs Munro lived up the glen in the last croft at Suledale, just beyond Chrissie's. They had a cow, which produced the most delicious fresh milk, which she brought down to the house each morning.

There was a track, which ran past the house right down to the shore, where the brothers Neil and Ronald Bethune used to row a ferry across the loch to Kingsburgh opposite. This was much quicker than having to go right round the loch.

Neil, who had a huge blackhead on his nose, beside his beard, was married. His brother, Ronald slept in the barn attached to the end of the house and used to collect bracken for his bed. The Bethunes used to supply us with the most wonderful deep red coloured eggs from their chickens, which had been feeding on seaweed and the like from the shore.

My younger brother, Alasdair, and I made a Commando Jump by running down the slope of the track past the house and across the road and the burn below it. It was quite a test, but that seemed to be the sort of thing we were always up to. We were always outside and usually went out as soon as it was daylight - in the boat or out on the hill. I remember one occasion when the police called to enquire why all the insulators on the telegraph poles near the house had been smashed and we had to admit guilt. I can't remember what the punishment was, but shooting them with a .22 was very satisfactory and great target practice. Vandalism started at an early age I fear.

My father with Alasdair, me and Ewan, Tayinloan Lodge 1946

There was always some sort of adventure or something to explore. In those days there was an aura and a spell that is less obvious today. There was a great feeling of time past and history..... a pace of life that had evolved relatively slowly until that time.

We had no electricity at Tayinloan then, but we did have Calor gas that made a strange hissing sound when it was lit and of course there were always the paraffin lamps and candles. Lighting the lamps had to be done slowly because the glass funnel would crack if you did it too fast. Lamplight and gas created a wonderfully peaceful sense in the house.

This disappeared with the arrival of a Lucas Freelight system. This was installed on the roof, with a propeller driving a dynamo. It managed to light a few bulbs and must have been one of the first wind turbines on Skye. At Skeabost there was a much bigger hydro scheme, which provided the lights and just enough electricity for a one bar electric fire.

Our telephone involved a party line, which we shared with Lyndale and two others. Sometimes one would hear heavy breathing on the line and we would say "Now stop listening in John", to which the reply would come "I'm no listening in Mr Ruaraidh", and the line would clear.

John Munro, brother of Hector, our gardener, ran the Post Office in Bernisdale and he would have to deliver a telegram by bicycle. That involved pushing it down the first part of the road to Treaslane because his bicycle had no brakes. He would mount his bicycle for the next bit which was flat for a few hundred yards. Then he would get off and push his bicycle up the next hill. At the top, it would be pushed downhill again to the house. All that meant a good dram was usually the cost of a delivery. Return to Bernisdale was then of course great fun to watch.

The telephone exchange and Post Office at Skeabost was run by the genial Ranald, with a wonderful peat smoke smell about it. I am sorry to say that it was fun to talk to him and then try to distract him so that you could pull out the telephone plugs and put them back in the wrong hole. He would get furious and we would then have to run for it.

The journey to Skye always had to involve the ferry, firstly at Ballachulish, then at Dornie and finally Kyle, which was always a great adventure. There were other ferries at Kylerhea or Stromeferry if we came that way. All the ferries had turntables, which took four large cars or a couple of lorries when full. On arrival at the slip one had to drive down the slope to get on board, the turntable was then revolved and off we set across the swirling tide with a lovely old Kelvin petrol/paraffin engine making its unmistakeable sounds. You were then able to drive straight off up the slip on the other side.

The roads were little more than tracks in places, often with grass in the middle, although there was always someone posted on each section whose job it was to mend the potholes. I remember my father telling me that the first cars to come on to Skye used to have to go up the hills backwards, because there were no petrol pumps in the early cars and so the petrol could not reach the carburettor by gravity. There were very few cars on the island in my youth so any time we passed someone walking along, we would usually stop to offer a lift.

Tayinloan was not really in a very good spot, for it had had to be built by the roadside for the stagecoach, and so it had no real views. But it was a very happy house and holds wonderful memories for me. The house is still there, even less visible now, as it has all become terribly overgrown, the trees have been allowed to get very tall, and the rhododendrons have taken over the garden. The same track still winds down to the shore, where the Bethune's croft is now an abandoned boathouse.

***

As I grew older, I spent more time out on the hill with my gun, stalking, or fishing in the loch.

I was given my first gun, by Grandad MacLeod when I was nine years old. He made a great fuss of presenting me with the 28 bore shotgun on the doorstep of Skeabost for my ninth birthday, and on 12th August 1936 I shot two and a half brace of grouse, a duck and a snipe. I think the duck was probably out of season but that was overlooked in the excitement. I still have the photograph, which reminds me constantly of those magic days.

12th August 1936 with my grandfather

I remember being allowed to come down for dinner on my first twelfth of August. Grandad MacLeod made it a great occasion and made me feel terribly important. But I was not allowed out on my own with a gun until I could recite confidently:

Never, never let your gun
Pointed be at anyone
All the pheasants ever bred
Won't repay for one man dead.
When a fence or hedge you cross,
Though of time it cause a loss,
From the gun the cartridge take,
For the greater safety's sake...

...And on it went. A well-loved verse, which remains a valuable foundation lesson for anyone learning to shoot at any age today.

As my father wasn't around for much of the time during the war, I used to go shooting with my younger brother Alasdair and we usually got back for breakfast by about nine o'clock, but I think we were often on the go from about six in the morning. It didn't take long to get a rabbit or two, then skin it and chop it up into six bits as bait for the lobster pots, which we could do before breakfast. Out of six pots you could be pretty certain of getting three or four lobsters every day as well as a few crabs; and we could live pretty well on them.

Sometimes I was asked to shoot a stag for the venison by Alec Edward, who lived at Sanquhar House near Forres. He had built the Dallas Dhu distillery there (his fourth distillery) and used to rent Kinloch Lodge, with its deer forest, during the war. The Lodge was old Lord Macdonald's shooting lodge and as a self-made man Alec Edward had much in common with my grandfather Duncan MacLeod, who had also built up his own whisky fortune from nothing. When Alec Edward was at Kinloch and wanted some venison for the house, he would call up Grandad and say "Send the boy down". Usually I would go with Jock Urquhart, but once I took Alasdair, who had never shot a stag before.

We spied all the ground and did not see anything possible, but on the way home I heard a roar on the hill above the Lodge. We left the path down by the shore and climbed up to have a look and there he was with his hinds; Alasdair had a shot and to my great excitement it fell. I was really happy because my brother and I had done the stalking and here was Alasdair's first stag. I stuck my knife into his neck to bleed it, but without getting a grip of his horn. Suddenly he leapt up and threw me back a couple of yards, puncturing my lung in the process.

The shot had hit the horn and stunned him, so he was actually fully alive but unconscious. When I tried to bleed him, it bought him round with a rude shock. I still have the hole today; not that it did me any harm.

I remember one time when my father came into my bedroom very early to wake me to say that there was an expedition to the island of Raasay to shoot woodcock and would I like to come? I leapt out of bed at once for we had to catch the steamer, which left Portree at eight, and what an exciting day that was. There was snow on the ground and that sunny island magic pervaded the senses, even when I was so young. I can still conjure it all up again as I write.

I started fishing with a rod at about the same time as I started shooting. Rationing limited what was available, so we could usually do pretty well with something from the sea or the hill. At that time one could go out in the launch with hand lines and come back with up to a hundred haddock, or "haddies" as they were known, in a couple of hours fishing. There are, of course, no haddock left today, because foreign trawlers have come in and scraped the bottom of all the lochs, ruining the prawn stocks on which the haddock used to feed. I suppose there was the odd trawler before, but they never came right inshore as they do now.

We used to go to the shore and dig for cockles at low tide, which were delicious to eat, but we really needed them for bait on the hand lines. Fishing with a hand line was tremendously exciting, as you would anchor the boat on a bank that had been identified from two opposing marks on the land. The hand line had two hooks hanging from each end of a 12 inch bit of heavy wire, with a chunk of lead suspended from the centre. It had to be dropped down until it hit the bottom. You would then lift it about one yard, so that the hooks would be just off the bottom and when something took the bait, you gave it a good jerk to hook the fish; and with luck, a couple of lovely fresh haddies were on board. There were just two or three places where you could drop anchor and fish but there are none today. I went out recently to try the old bank and could not get anything at all.

We used to fish for mackerel and cuddies with a fixed line and a large white fly on a long bamboo pole which was held on your shoulder with the tip of the pole held down into the water. There would be a long plank placed across the stern of a rowing boat to sit on facing backwards while Hector would row. When you had a bite, up came the pole and you had to catch the swinging fish and un-hook it. Small lythe, (or pollack as they are sometimes known) and saithe which are rather bony and not as good, are all known as cuddies.

When we had a good catch, we would always distribute some to neighbours, and as we usually had a few people in the house they never seemed to last long. Everyone found fresh fish for breakfast absolutely delicious.

***

After many attempts to persuade him to let me try my first pipe, when I was about 13, Hector Munro finally gave me a smoke with Bogie Roll. It was a stick of compressed green tobacco from which he had to cut bits off to scrunch up in the palm of his hand. He then stuffed this dreadful mixture into the bowl of the pipe. When he lit it a cloud of lethal smoke ensued with a sort of gurgling sound. When I tried it, I shall never forget the ghastly retching that followed and I really was a very chastened boy!

On one occasion during the war, a section of landing craft, that had been carried on the deck of a cargo ship torpedoed by a German submarine in the Minch, floated into the loch. It had an anchor hanging down so that it stopped just opposite Kingsburgh, where my Aunt Isa and Cousin Colin Campbell lived. I was out in the launch with Alasdair and Ewan, doing the lobster pots, when we spied this potential prize and decided to have a good look. We managed to get a line on to it, boarded and discovered that it had all sorts of goodies like tins of petrol (rationed at that time), cans of tinned fruit, anti-foul paint etc., so we scooped up as much as we could carry. A few days later, out again in the launch, the wind got up just as our rudder broke and we started to drift towards the Kingsburgh shore. As we neared the hulk, we noticed that there were people on board the wreck, so we called for a line and some assistance to which an American voice replied: "not unless you return the stolen goods!" Protestations of innocence were of no avail, for we had spilled some of the anti-foul paint on the rocks beside the slip where we kept the dinghy, and we were now quite close to the rocks, so I shouted "OK, I will see what we can do".

They threw us a line and after rather a difficult conversation, we agreed to get them some fresh chicken in return for being let "off the hook". Now this was a bit of a problem, so we decided that Lyndale was the place to raid. Aunt Gay had her chickens in the wood near the house and we should be able to pinch one or two without being seen.

Very stupidly, having caught two or three, we plucked and gutted them nearby, but of course the traces we left did not look like the work of a fox or otter. The booty got us clear of the Americans on the hulk, but then landed us in big trouble when the crime was traced. I don't think Aunt Gay ever forgave me for leading that little op, for the atmosphere thereafter with her was always a bit tense.

My mother used to come out on the boat occasionally. Mostly for a picnic, but I never thought of her as much of a doer. My mother loved it if we caught something. She had a cook, but she was a very good hostess and always kept menus in a book that she retained for the purpose.

***

I did once get a fright, which is why I do not go out on the hill by myself now. I had climbed up and was going to stalk down onto a stag, which was down a gully with a lot of stones and rocks in it. In the course of the stalk I got into a position out of which I could only get by either stepping on a piece of grass which I thought might hold my weight, or by climbing up a very steep rock face, which looked sort of impossible, while carrying a rifle and wearing rubber boots.

As I stepped onto this bit of grass it gave way and I shot down the steep rocky slope, taking all the skin off my hands. I managed to hold the rifle in front of me while descending, hoping that I was not going to hit something at the bottom. Actually I managed to get the stag, because he didn't hear me, I can't quite think how. But I thought to myself then – you are a bloody fool because no one knows where you are - or even that I was out by myself. I was a long way away from the road and no hope of any help had I bust my leg or something. It was exciting and fun to go out by myself but second thoughts prevailed after that incident.

I used to stalk at Eileanreach every year with Judy Dulverton. Ian Campbell was the stalker. We were quite high up once and had to walk along a ledge on the edge of a precipice to get in. There was a very big drop below us just to the right, and a tuft of grass, which Ian put his left foot on, and as I was following, I put my right foot on the same spot which gave way. I shot down the face of the cliff, twenty feet or so, and bust my nose in the process. I was covered in blood and my hands were a bit scratched, but I stopped on a ledge and looked up to see Ian's absolutely horrified face looking to see his "gentleman" had survived. He shot down after me, coming down like a goat. "Are you alright, sir?

Are you alright?" he said. I was actually perfectly alright although a bit battered, so he helped me up the cliff and we got in and shot the stag. Ian was very tickled with that.

Ian was great fun. These men who spend their lives on the hills and run the stalking are wonderful "salt of the earth" sort of people and I remember coming back off the hill with Ian one day, when he stopped by a rock and asked if I could lift another rock beside the first one and put it down on top of the other one, which had a bit of an indentation on it. The rock he was pointing to was large and round. It was very difficult to get a grip of it. I tried to lift it but it was very awkward and heavy, and I just could not do it. I asked him if he could do it and why he wanted me to try to which he said, in days gone by, if a man wanted to take a certain lady to be his bride, he would take her up to the rock, and if she could lift it, he would marry her.

I thought that was absolutely splendid for in those days of course, the women did all the heavy work, carrying in the peats and the water, while the menfolk were fishing or working the land!

I used to stalk at Benula every year with Iain Tennant and that was always great fun. The house was just below the dam at the beginning of Loch Mullardoch and we had to sail right up the loch before you could get onto the hill. He had a huge great big fat stalker called Gibson who was pretty useless, with Kenny as his number two. Kenny subsequently went to Perry Fairfax after he had bought Benula from Iain. It was always wonderful to return back down the loch in the evening, with maybe two or three stags in the dingy, and a bottle of whisky on the coach house roof of the launch, soaking wet and the sun setting behind us. Great days.

CHAPTER TWO

Schooldays

I was about seven years old when I first ran away from school. It was called St Neots and I hated it. But I remember feeling very relieved when I was later found, in a lane with trees on either side, by somebody in a car and taken home.

At my next school, Sandroyd, King Peter of Yugoslavia was in my dormitory in one bed with his guard outside. His father was assassinated and King Peter had to leave suddenly which rather saddened me for he was a kindly person. He had a younger brother called Prince Tomislav, a little younger than me, but a pleasant chap nevertheless.

My father and his brothers had been to Sandroyd and had been successful both academically and on the games field, but I was always being punished for something or other, usually with a cane or a slipper.

This continued until one day on a Sunday walk, I was lagging behind the group when a prefect called de Peirera told me to hurry up. He was flicking the back of my bare legs with a stick so I told him that if he did that again I would hit him. He did and I hit him, rather effectively I think for he had a broken nose and lots of blood.

That evening my Father came down and sat on the end of my bed in the dormitory. Gently and rather ashamedly, he told me that I had to leave the school. I leapt out of bed with a whoop of sheer delight, for I could not believe that this ghastly experience was to end. De Pereira later became a Spanish Ambassador, I believe.

The Headmaster was called Mr Ozanne and I can still smell the aura of his hair oil.

There was a school ditty, which ran "Mr Ozanne is a very good man, he goes to church on Sundays. He prays to God to give him strength, to beat the boys on Mondays." Leaving Sandroyd was one of the happiest moments of my youth.

My Father had been at the school with Ronald Hornby, a charming and kindly man who ran a much smaller school in Hampshire called Emsworth House. His wife Margot was a dear and they had a small daughter called Tessa (who married George Ramsay of the Scots Guards in later life). I had been thinking of joining the Navy at that time and Emsworth House was considered suitable, but it was a far more pleasant school where I only got into relatively infrequent trouble. I settled in and in due course managed to pass into Eton, taking Middle Fourth without any great difficulty.

During all this time my parents had been renting various houses in England for fairly short periods, starting with Boveney Court, a delightful old house belonging to Eton College. The chief memory I have of that house was of my father's brother, Uncle Goo, coming down to see us in his Bentley and a peacock standing on the bonnet. We managed to feed it grapes, which we could watch fascinated, slipping down the bird's throat.

Then came Sandford Manor, Waltham St Lawrence, which had the River Loddon running though the field in front of the house. There was a boathouse with a punt and a canoe in it and I can remember putting one of the Skye cousins into the punt and then shoving it out into the river, followed by screams of terror. I can't remember the punishment.

There was a road bridge over the river and I had just learned to swim with water wings I think. The challenge was to try climbing across it on the wrong side, for there was a narrow ledge on the outside. About half way over I fell off into the water, just beside a post that was jutting up and I recall the relief of missing it. Then I had to swim without the water wings and made the bank panting and rather frightened.

My brother Alasdair had run off to get help for me but of course that just resulted in another punishment. I cannot remember how long we stayed at Sandford Manor, but we moved to Woodlands Park, Great Missenden, just before the war and I think that must have just about coincided with my time at Emsworth House. At that time my Father had the 8 Litre Bentley GN 1869 which had a silver plaque on the dashboard with the engine number, chassis number and the weight inscribed on it (it was two tons 15 cwt). My parents took the Bentley on a classic journey from Portree to Dubrovnik right after dancing two nights at the Skye balls in 1937.

Woodlands Park had a lovely walled garden and nice gardener called Reynolds, or Mr Reynolds as we called him. He lived in a cottage by the garden and then there was Perry who drove the Bentley sometimes, in uniform.

Perry lived in a cottage at the top of a nearby hill in the grounds, and on the drive there was a cattle grid with two sets of bars over a pit. I had a toboggan on wheels called a "flexy racer" and it was tremendous fun to shoot down the drive, over the cattle grid if one had enough momentum. Another fun thing was to hide in the pit and watch Harrods van cross over, particularly if we had put sugar in the petrol tank. We always hoped that something exciting would happen, but of course, it never did. The poor driver probably had to walk for miles after the engine stopped; we never heard.

Near Woodlands Park was the house belonging to the Mead family where there was a squash court and I used to play squash with the son. I had a tutor for the holidays called Robert Graves. He was a master at Sandroyd and later became rather famous as a poet. We got him to come and play squash, rather reluctantly. At a suitable moment I made an excuse to go outside and we locked him in. There was a fearful stink when he managed to escape, but we got rid of him, which was the main objective. Robert Graves was hired to teach me Latin; he had curly red hair and was very tall. I disliked him heartily, probably because he was trying to teach me Latin.

Even at that age I was uncomfortable with convention and there was a good deal of that in my childhood. My father had a very traditional approach to life, which was splendid in some ways, but I didn't feel it suited me.

Throughout all this time the main summer holidays were always in Skye, with some winter holidays too. Skye always seemed to be the real home, although my Mother was a genius at making the house wherever we were, comfortable and homely.

*****

In the summer of 1939 I went to Eton, dressed in a tailcoat, top hat and equipped with all the necessities for one's own room. An Ottoman and a basket chair were essentials, with photographs of the parents, some pictures by Peter Scott, the wildlife artist and son of Captain Scott of the Antarctic, whom I admired tremendously.

My Eton housemaster, Bill Marsden, was a sort of ogre, very tall and gangly and with a messy moustache, and he smoked a pipe that sounded as if he was filtering the smoke though spittle. His reputation was terrifying as was his nickname of "Bloody Bill". He used to play pocket billiards with his balls while he talked and he knew Bradshaw's guide to the train timetables by heart.

My first few days were awful. I had to learn all the different House colours, find out where I had to be at what time and discover pretty well all of this with very little help. Very gradually, I learned the layout and soon discovered that life at Eton was run by the boys and you were treated as an adult.

Masters were necessary for lessons only, but all the discipline in the House was managed by the Library, a band of the senior five or six boys in the House. "Pop" was a remote school police force of God-like figures with extremely fancy waistcoats and spongebag trousers. They were responsible for all the main school discipline. Woe betide anyone who crossed their path. The President of Pop, Justin Mackeurtan was also Captain of my House, Marsdens, and the spell he cast was considerable.

That first "half', (as a term at Eton was called), I made friends with Johnny MacRae who boarded at Mays House, across the road from Marsdens. We decided it would be a good scheme to puncture all the tyres of the cars outside Lower Chapel, by setting a nail fore and aft under each wheel of several cars. Something prompted us, I can't remember what; we were after a particular car probably, but as we had a bag of nails, we thought, let's get the lot...!

The resulting chaos was watched with a mixture of wonder and trepidation. Retribution was to follow, inevitably in the form of a "round robin" to every House at Eton; "Who done it?" Johnny owned up but I kept quiet and would not have been found out had my conscience not let me down. Johnny got "Pop tanned" and I was beaten in the House by Justin Mackeurtan, with more or less the same ignominy. I don't think I'm very proud of that incident. It reminds me of rule number one. It doesn't matter what you do so long as you don't get caught.

Life at Eton continued on the edge as it were, with Bill Marsden becoming more and more of a friend, following crime and punishment. His terrifying exterior covered up a secret admiration for "crime" as he saw it. I suppose that he really did enjoy beating me; for unlike any other Housemaster, who simply left discipline to the Library in their House, Bill would take the law into his own hands and dispense justice in his own way. This had many advantages for it kept the lid on scandal, away from the public gaze, and it enabled one to "exchange" the standard punishment of "lines" for a thrashing that was over and done with quickly.

For instance, I was irritating a new science master, Captain Davies, by swinging a blind chord against the window during his class. Every time I did it he made a mark on his desk and at the end of the school, he called me in and gave me a "ticket" which was a bit of paper with my punishment written on it, for signature by my Housemaster and Classical Tutor. The penalty imposed was to be my reciting Paradise Lost by the following day. Quite impossible I thought, so I asked Bill if he would exchange it. His eye lit up and he said "Well, that is a very big task. It's worth at least 12." "That is too many" I said. "I'll take 6". "No, no. It's worth much more than 6. Make it 10". "No Sir" I said. "If you make it 8, I'll accept" and so it was. I am sure that he enjoyed the encounter and I got off a very tiresome time indeed.

On one occasion, soon after my brother Alasdair arrived in the Easter half, Stoke Poges Golf Course was flooded and then frozen over. Ice hockey was possible and Bill had said that he would take anybody interested in his ancient open Talbot, provided that we were ready by, say, two o'clock.

Alasdair was late and so we missed the transport. I hired a taxi, which was illegal at Eton. We managed to park the taxi and join the ice hockey through a hedge, imagining that we had arrived unseen by Bill. That evening he came into my room and said that he had not seen us on the transport. "You must have taken a taxi" he said and after some rather weak denials, I said "Oh well, I suppose we did". "Well" said Bill, "I'll give you a choice. You can have a thrashing from me now and skate tomorrow, or you can give up skating tomorrow." Naturally, I chose the former and the following day it thawed and skating was off. He visited me again after that and said "You made the wrong choice then", and laughed to himself I'm sure. Certainly I did after the state of my backside had settled.

Bill had a great sense of humour, although he didn't look as though he had. He was quite a threatening figure and used to frighten the life out of some people. But he seemed to me to have a sporting instinct. I think he secretly enjoyed the things one got up to.

I had a "crib" for the Latin construe bound up in a cover of The White Company, a Conan Doyle novel. I kept it in a shop in the High Street called Devereux, with Hazel who used to look after the top hats. Every morning I used to do the Latin construe from the crib in the shop and it was a fool proof system. One morning I was pushed for time and so took the crib into school with me. I returned to the House for lunch and put the crib into the pocket of my overcoat, which I hung up on my door. After lunch I went for a run and after a few moments realised that I had left the crib in my room. Bill was prone to look for contraband while one was out, thinking that we did not know, and so I returned hotfoot to find it gone. Nothing was said for several days and then he called me in. There was the crib on his desk and he said, "What is this?"

"Well," I said "it's a very good book that I've not had time to read yet. I like Conan Doyle and wonder what you think of him?".

"It's a crib" he said and informed me that I would be beaten.

On recovering my breath, I returned to his room and said "you know that I have been depending on this crib for the whole half, and if you take it away from me now, I shall fail in Trials", the examinations that came at the end of each term.

"If you promise not to cheat any more, I will give it back to you," he said and he did. For me too it was a matter of honour that I respected, and indeed did not cheat again. I suppose he gave it back because he thought I would fail and he hated failure. I didn't much like it either. I was a good student. I never had any trouble with work. I cruised through but I never did more than I absolutely had to.

Bill had that insight into my character that I respected and came to love. He would have done anything for one of his boys and I'm sure that we would have done the same for him. He was a wonderful man who would not have been able to exercise his touch today.

I had ninepence a day to spend at school, which meant you had to save up to get two and sixpence! That was the order one had at Rowlands, which was the place one used to go and feast to compensate for the somewhat limited wartime rations.

Sixpence a day was about the cheapest anyone got. There were some very poor boys getting this. Very rich boys got one and sixpence a day. I don't think you were meant to have much more than this. I suppose we went and brought ice cream. Mrs White made lobster fishcakes in her shop, quite a long way up Eton High Street, which cost one and sixpence each. They were absolutely delicious and reminded me of Skye. I suppose there was just enough money, but not a lot.

One crime, I can't remember what, bought me up against the headmaster, Claude Elliot. We had pre-military training before leaving school and were climbing on the lead-roofed dome of School Hall where

I met the headmaster on the top. He had come up from the other side. He was a lovely man who spoke in a rather curious, stilted way. "Oh," he said. "What are you doing here?" It was very difficult to get started because the roof was so steep but then it got easier. It was normally against the rules, but you were allowed to climb it if you were about to join the army. Elliott used to come to Skye to climb The Cuillins so for once I did not get into trouble.

Beatings always used to take place after prayers, which followed supper, after which you went to your room to work, or whatever. That was when someone in The Library would shout "Boy!" in a loud voice, whereupon all the lower boys had to run. The last boy to arrive at The Library would be told to go and get Hilleary.

Hilleary would then know that he was in trouble. The form was you had to bend down and put your head under the desk whereupon The Captain of the House had a go at you with a cane, usually up to about ten thrashes.

If you wanted to be clever you could get a silk handkerchief and make a bacon sandwich with another silk handkerchief, which could be put inside your trousers to make the same sound as your backside. The trouble was, if you got more than about six, the bacon would break up and start leaking through the back of your trousers; and if you were caught "padding", as it was called, you had to take it out and then get some more. I was not usually padded because I never had time to get it ready.

I was probably beaten every other week, on average. Usually for work, I think, but I would prefer not to remember. Tim Gilpin was the only Captain of the House who never beat me, but I suppose I was fair game, because it really did not bother me. I was finally elected to The Library at the very end, just before I left Eton.

I was never much in fear of authority figures but I didn't enjoy Eton and was pretty unhappy there. It was such a huge conventional place where one was supposed to wear a top hat and tailcoat and obey all the rules. I had been given the choice of Gordonstoun at one point but I knew nothing at all about it, although it did sound much more like my kind of form. I think I would probably have been far better off there but my parents wanted Eton and so that is where I went.

There was certainly a great standard of excellence there, and people like my brother-in-law, Jackie Shaw Stewart, who was very clever, went into College, which separated them from the riff raff like me. They were all known as "Tugs" and were looked down upon as inferior beings by "Oppidans", as ordinary boys were called.

***

I only had one term of peace before the war came. All the bigger boys joined up and many of them were killed. I remember thinking - I wish I could get involved in this.

I joined the Eton Corps as soon as I could, although I can't remember when exactly. I do remember being bet that I could not drink 20 glasses of water before a Corps parade on one occasion, which resulted in my needing to pee really badly, on parade. I can't remember the Company Sergeant Major's name but he was rather deaf, or at least pretended to be, so that when I asked to be excused, nothing happened. Disaster! I think I took the initiative eventually and had to wait for ages before I could do anything, which of course resulted in a good bollocking when I did manage to return.

Date stones would fit into the old .303 rifles quite well so that when fired by a blank cartridge it made a pretty fearsome missile. I am not very proud of having shot at the Adjutant's horse in Windsor Great Park on a field day; it was Reggie Colquhoun I think, and he took off rather satisfactorily in a cloud of dust.

I was not a very keen soldier at that time, (Scots Guards and SAS came later), and so I transferred to the Air Training Corps. "Codger" Kerry was a Housemaster in command of the Corps. He had arranged for flying lessons to be available at Booker aerodrome, not far from school, so it was quite easy to bicycle there. Of course I made friends with my instructor very smartly and he offered to give me extra lessons, unofficially. Consequently, I used to go to Booker aerodrome on half-holiday Wednesday afternoons. I became pretty good at flying until one day Kerry followed me, discovered my enterprise and hauled me up. He accused me of "taking advantage". I did not think that was the sort of attitude I expected from the RAF, so I resigned.

I was quite successful on the river for I could row well and was very strong. I was eventually put in The Eight. But the coach, Tom Brocklebank, disliked me intensely, which was entirely mutual, so he sacked me for being a nuisance and I was relegated to The Second Eight. We were allowed to go to the famous Henley Regatta where we raced against The Eight and beat them in a practice run which really pleased me.

Eton at that time took a mixture of academic standards and not just the cleverest, as seems to happen today. My brother Ewan, for instance, took Third Form, which was right at the bottom. I was in the middle. Not up at the top, but certainly not at the bottom either.

***

The steamer Loch Nevis used to travel from Portree, via Raasay to Kyle and Mallaig. We used it on our journey back to Eton at the end of the school holidays.

If we came by bus and ferry from Portree to Kyle, Pollock's lorry would meet the ferry and transport the heavy luggage up to the train station.

Tormod (Sir Torquhil later) Matheson was slightly older than me and his younger brother Fergus slightly younger; both of them were huge boys. They used to join us at Duirinish, where they lived. Behaviour on the train between Kyle and Inverness was pretty terrible. On one occasion I remember Tormod, who was Captain of the Boats, and a sort of God at school, had a pipe. He lit the pipe and put its bowl in his mouth and the stem through the door. He closed the door on the stem and blew a lot of smoke out into the corridor. It filled with smoke and the guard came along thinking the train was on fire. When he finally got to the source of the fire, Tormod put his foot against the door and shut it against the guard. They should have thrown us off the train really.

Then there were the paper cups - probably made by Mono Containers, the company my father had worked for - in a dispenser for drinking water in the loo. If you filled one with water and crimped the end over, it could be thrown it at the stationmaster as he went past. It was simply inexcusable vandalism. That's why one was always getting caught and beaten. But it seemed to be rather fun and I suppose being destructive had an early attraction. Destroying things seemed to be very satisfactory.

Skye and Lochalsh were "number one protected areas" during the war and you needed a permit to travel through on the train. Once, on our way home from school we were not allowed through because a Royal Navy boat, the Port Napier, filled with mines, had caught fire in the port at Kyle. We had to sit on the train for a day while they scuttled the boat. The Port Napier is still in the harbour, but at the bottom.

War was declared in the summer holidays of my first term at Eton and we were constantly aware of being quite close to London for the bombing there.

We felt the war arrived at Eton the night a bomb landed on the music master's house in School Yard, just opposite College. The house was destroyed, but fortunately the music master, Daddy Lee, was out. He was a nice little fat man. That bomb brought the war a bit closer.

A lot of friends were killed just after they left Eton. There was quite a shocking turnover like that. The first one of the older boys to be killed was John Currie for which I was very sad. But then there was always something dramatic happening with war in the background.

Winston Churchill's speeches were enormously inspiring like "We will fight them on the beaches" and that sort of stuff, and as a boy, I was full of admiration for that kind of leadership and the idea that this small island was not going to be defeated.

You could summarise it by saying that school in general was a pretty good failure for me although I never actually failed at anything at school. The war was on, the quality of some of the masters had dropped a bit because so many of the good ones had gone off to fight. I used to say that it was a complete waste of money going to a boarding school. And that it was far better to go to the local school, and then make it up at home or afterwards. But I'm not sure if I'd stand by that now.

War was definitely a frightening prospect. I used to keep my Mannlicher rifle under the bed at home and was hoping the Germans were going to land and one wondered how afraid one would be. There was certainly much talk of the invasion and a whole lot of people left the country for Canada. I don't think I admired that much, but there was certainly a fear that the Germans would land and how would one fight? It did seem that fighting underground would be essential.

April 19 1944

Eton College
Windsor
Dear Hilleary,

I am afraid that these reports are rather late, but I am rather exhausted at the end of the half, and brought them away.

I have parted from Ruaraidh with great regret, not only that 5 years of rough and tumble have come to an end, but also that I don't feel that he has steadied himself as much as I had hoped for a year ago.

It has been an uphill struggle, and I thought a year ago that his foot was fairly firmly planted, but something has gone wrong each half, and I have not the confidence in his judgement and direction for which I perhaps optimistically had hoped.

There are many good qualities in him chiefly perhaps a sunny and friendly nature which is seldom (though sometimes) dashed by temper or depression: he never bears any malice, but he rather expects to be treated as a "special case", from whom normal achievements cannot be expected: he has some wits but is very loth to use them consciously, and least of all in the way that is mapped out for him: he realises that he is not a scholar, not unnaturally, but he has not enough confidence in the powers of mind that he has, and assumes "that it is all beyond him", when as a matter of fact he can apply his common sense quite effectively: he knows he has made mistakes, as he has, and so distrusts his capacity.

However, his immediate future will call for a different kind of intelligence, and one where he may feel more confidence, and I don't see why he should not acquit himself quite well in the military life: but as I said and have told him, lapses of discipline and errors of "contact" will cost him more than he can afford, and he will not be able to wipe the slate clean in a moment as he can at school.

His early years at Eton were difficult, and he had no friends - apart from some bad lots, who have fallen by the way: and he might well have followed them! But the last 3 years or so he has been on good terms with most people, boys and masters alike: as an individual he has been really liked, as indeed his human qualities entitle him, but always with a qualification that "you will never be sure he will not go off the deep end in some way": and that is the last word of warning that I can give him, to keep his ballast and think twice before breaking obviously fresh ice.

I hope and expect that he will steady down: and the rigid discipline of the Guards will either do the trick or will break him: and I think he has enough stuff in him not to let the second alternative happen.

I do not want to end on a gloomy note, for despite inevitable disagreements, he has never really quarrelled and it is just as much to his credit as to mine that he has been able to weather his time at Eton without ill feeling.

He leaves here with all our good wishes for the future, and I hope we shall often see him.

Yours sincerely
H K Marsden (Bloody Bill)

CHAPTER THREE

War and the Scots Guards

I was accepted for a commission in the Scots Guards by Col. Bill Balfour at an interview with him at 11am from Eton, early in 1944. He was an imposing figure behind a huge desk with a decanter of port on view. He asked me to come in and sit down and asked if I would like a glass of port, which I accepted eagerly. My grandfather had had Crofts 1912 and Taylors 1908 circulating at Skeabost, so I thought I would try it on and said "Is this the '08 Sir?" By chance I had the correct year and as a result he never asked me another question. I was in!

Lt Ruaraidh Hilleary Scots Guards 1945

I joined the Brigade Squad in May 1944 at Caterham and became a recruit leader with David Ogilvy (now Airlie), Bill Macpherson (now Sir William of Cluny) and Mike Shaw Stewart. Geoffrey Rossiter was a Jewish old Etonian friend in our squad, with long, black hair. When he sat down in the barber's chair the barber said to him - "How would you like it cut, sir", with his tongue in his cheek. Geoffrey said - "Well, don't take too much off the sides and not too much off the top please". The barber then took the mowing machine approach and went straight over the top and giving him a full crew cut. I shall never forget the look on his face as he looked at his long, black locks on the floor.

We were put through the most extraordinary tests for long-suffering tolerance, and made to do all sort of absurdities. But the war was on and we felt we were getting ready to go somewhere and do something, so somehow it seemed to make good sense.

We were never given a moment's peace. We were woken up at crack of every dawn and chased every minute of the day so that you never, ever touched the ground. We had to run everywhere and if you were caught walking anywhere, you were in big trouble so we became extremely fit. And as one was young and quite able to do it, it was all rather fun.

I remember when the sergeant used the word "fuck", we laughed, for I don't think we had ever heard the word before. It was never used in quite the sense that it is now. Every other word came out like that which we thought really funny, but they really thought we would be frightened when threatened with this awful word.

Caterham lasted for six weeks, during which time David Ogilvy and I were thrown out of the Hammersmith Palais de Dance for attending in hobnail boots. Trained Soldier Atkinson was an old sweat, appointed to supervise our Platoon. He drew up all the kit with which we were supposed to be issued, such as yellow dusters, shoe polish etc., and then sold them to us.

On one memorable occasion Sgt. Veitch was giving us a weapon training lesson when a doodlebug landed about 50 yards away making a huge bang. He gave us a great bollocking for not paying attention and that was a fine example of how to behave under fire. Whenever a doodlebug cut out at an angle of some 45 degrees or so, one started to anticipate trouble. Whenever that happened at night trained Soldier Atkinson would be the first one under the bed.

***

After Caterham I spent 12 weeks at Pirbright, in a potential officers platoon, before attending the War Office Selection Board (WOSB) where one had to answer a lot of silly questions as they looked to see if you had officer potential. I passed and then went to the Mons barracks for officer training.

I was commissioned into the Scots Guards from Mons barracks in February 1945 and then returned to Pirbright as a young officer. On my first day in the officer's mess, in my brand new uniform from Saville Row and all sorts of new kit, I was met by Andy Drummond Moray, an old, and very senior, major. He gave David and me, and one or two other new officers a lecture about how we were to carry on. The one impression he made on me was that a young officer in the Brigade of Guards never calls a major "Sir" and should always be addressed by his first name. The commanding officer was addressed as "Sir" once during the day, but otherwise he should be called Colonel Bill or Colonel Fred, or whoever he was. These terribly senior people were old enough to be my father, so it was all a bit of a shock.

After Pirbright I was then attached to Jonathan Cory-Wright's platoon, which shortly afterwards was posted to the Scots Guards Battle School near Carnaervon in North Wales. Everyone had to go through this battle school course. We were shot at with live ammunition and learned all about the real thing before being shunted abroad for action.

After we had been there for two or three days, it was Jonathan's turn to go abroad to join the 2nd Bn in France, but he was killed a week later. Bill Struthers, who had been commanding the Demonstration Platoon, took over Jonathan's platoon, but he was killed after about a fortnight.

I had taken over the Demonstration Platoon from Bill so after his death it was my turn to go to France, but the war came to an end on VE day. So I missed my turn only by a couple of weeks, to my eternal regret. Although I probably wouldn't have lasted long myself, for there were a lot of casualties at the end.

While I was still commanding the demonstration platoon, Michael Crichton-Stuart, who had been with the Long Range Desert Group (LRDG), arrived at the Battle School to say that an SAS unit was being formed to go to Burma and would I be interested? That was perhaps my first interest in the SAS, but it never happened, because the war in the Far East had also ended.

Bob Rivers-Bulkeley, who later became a great friend, was the commanding officer of the Battle School while I was there. He had been with David Stirling in the desert. Stirling had used the LRDG to navigate deep into the Sahara desert, to help the SAS reach inaccessible targets. In effect they became the taxi service for the early, deep raids into the Sahara.

A few months after VE day, I was posted to Right Flank of the 3rd Bn Scots Guards at Veiden, a village near Cologne, under Charles Graham. Peter Fane Gladwin had been the Training Major at Pirbright, and he considered David and me to be good young officers. He had been posted to the 3rd Bn very shortly after the end of the war with the brief to convert the 3rd Bn back to infantry, which involved getting rid of their tanks. They had been a most successful armoured Battalion and of course were deeply attached to their tanks, so Peter's arrival was not popular, and a write up for David and me was like the kiss of death.

We lived in amazing style at Veiden. A jeep used to be sent about 100 miles from the officer's mess to Brussels every other day to get champagne and oysters. The spoils of war were evident, some of which was "acquired" from locals, who were not allowed to have weapons. In fact I still have a gun here, which I acquired at that time.

Some of the Guardsmen behaved badly when they were drunk. One guardsman used to drink brake fluid, and of course that eventually killed him.

There was a lovely old Anglophile German aristocrat called Baron von Boeselegar whose family castle, Heimerzheim, was nearby. We used to go there to shoot. The Baron had had five sons, all killed on the Russian front, but he would invite us over and was tremendously hospitable. In the castle he had the world's record red deer stag's head. He had shot the stag in the Carpathian Mountains by calling it in with a sound like a roaring stag, through a parchment tube stuck in his mouth. He also had a silver model of this stag and a model of himself standing beside it and he was a big man who stood just about up to the stag's shoulder.

Heimerzheim shoots consisted of setting out to encircle a big area of perhaps a mile, with a gun followed by a beater and so on. The head keeper would blast on the horn, and everyone would converge, and there would be another blast on the horn for the guns to stop. The beaters would continue forward into the centre of the circle so that any partridges, hares and sometimes the odd boar would break out and be shot. One had to be careful not to shoot into the circle but only after game was breaking outwards. Sometimes we also shot driven wild boar with a rifle when they were driven through the woods.

It was an extraordinary time which lasted about six months, just after the end of the war. The only building left standing in Cologne after the allied bombings was the Cathedral. Practically the whole of the city was in ruins, so one of the jobs we had to do was to patrol the city through the night, to ensure that nobody was about until 4 am when the curfew ended and the population literally emerged from the rubble to queue for bread. All the houses had been destroyed and people were forced to live in the cellars.

The local civilian population was completely disorientated, but we did not see any of Germany's concentration camp horrors. The military were in control and were trying to produce an administration to get the country running again and literally re-build the bridges, such as the bridge over the river in Cologne which was, like the city, completely destroyed.

I revisited Cologne a few years ago and found that it had been completely rebuilt, and all the old buildings accurately restored.

I had a very nice black spaniel at that time, Snipe, acquired from old Baron von Boeselegar, for a pound of coffee; but very sadly Snipe was run over by a train as we left for the 1st Bn. in Trieste after the 3rd Bn. was disbanded.

The 3rd Bn Scots Guards had an interesting number of subsequently notable officers such as Willie Whitelaw, who became Margaret Thatcher's right-hand man; Bob Runcie, later Archbishop of Canterbury, Hector Laing who later ran United Biscuits, John Mann, Alasdair Gordon, Tony Stevenson and quite a few others too.

I was posted to Right Flank of the 1st Bn under Colin Dalrymple at Trieste with whom I remained until demobbed in 1947.

I was a fairly troublesome young officer I suppose. Peter Balfour, the adjutant, sentenced me to see the men's breakfast one day, but I failed to attend, so he gave me a colossal bollocking and a further month's punishment. That seemed pretty tough, but after it was completed, I marched in and said I wanted some leave, at which Peter asked me what I was going to do. I told him that I had turned the canvas canopy of a 15cwt truck back to front and put an old officer's mess arm chair in the back, and that I intended to tour Italy with Guardsman Hardiman as my driver. To my horror, Peter then asked if he could join me. So we arranged to put another armchair in the back and off we went. I can't imagine what this eccentric pair must have looked like, but to my surprise, we actually spent a most interesting leave together and it was a highly enjoyable trip.

While in Trieste the Battalion was responsible for patrolling the line, drawn by General Morgan between Yugoslavia and Italy to separate the two countries. We patrolled because the Yugoslavs, or Jugs as they were known then, were quite predatory towards the Italians. There was a lot of squabbling as to where the mark should be. Each country had two outposts along the line in various places. I was at one of the outposts, with David Moncreiff as my platoon commander. Because milk was in short supply, I had got myself a goat, Boadacia, to supply me with fresh milk. It was good clean, fresh milk, except that the guardsmen used to feed Boadacia cigarettes, which made the milk taste foul. One night, the Pipe Major cut its beard off and painted the poor thing with purple stripes!

I also had a goose called Caractacus, but it developed a taste for bread soaked in Cyprus brandy, which meant that the poor old thing became an alcoholic. It did still lay the odd egg though, which complemented the rations, which were otherwise pretty basic.

I never took any home leave from Italy, really so that I could climb in the summer and ski in the winter at Cortina, which was two hours away by car. My great friend, Rory Fraser and I did many climbs in the Dolomites together and what fun that always was. We wore very light felt shoes with suede tops for climbing on the very sharp rock. Cold tea in a flask was our usual drink, for it did get pretty hot in those magic hills and it was an excellent thirst-quencher.

Rory Fraser was the third son of Alasdair Fraser of Moniack, Shimi Lovat's cousin. He had been to Ampleforth. We had met in the Scots Guards, although he was slightly younger than me. He was a terrific enthusiast who loved climbing and I taught him to ski. On skis, he never wanted to turn a corner, so went absolutely straight down until he had a frightful crash. Then he would get up and set off again.

I learned to ski in Cortina. I had been to St Moritz in 1936 and watched the Cresta but they wouldn't let me do it as I was only nine years old at the time. I had not skied again until Cortina.

I had a guide there, Luciano de Bigontina who was young, fit, strong and enterprising and a simply lovely man. He always used to say – "Sempre Straight Down - don't bother turning corners". I used to do that and then have tremendous crashes, which got me christened "l'Inglese Rosso" - for getting very red in the face when I had crashed.

I took my grandson, Archie, and granddaughter, Iona, skiing a few years ago to Selva in Val Gardena. Archie and Iona were going to ski school in the morning, so I said that one day I would like them to be in ski school for the whole day while I went over to Cortina to see if I could find Luciano.

I went to the Carabinieri and asked if they could point out the Bigontina house, which used to be a rather poor peasant's farmhouse. Now though, it was a very smart chalet, with several floors, apartments and flats and "de Bigontina" marked on a sign for the ground floor. So I pressed the button and out came a woman. I introduced myself in my sketchy Italian, so she asked me in and there was Luciano seated on a sofa watching TV. He took one look at me and said: "L'Inglese Rosso!" as I came through the door and it was 50 years since we had met!

***

During the two years Rory Fraser and I were in Trieste we climbed a lot in Cortina. We had a guide called de Gasper who always used to say "no problem, no problem," when it was getting very hairy.

Adrian Seymour was the second in command of the battalion in Trieste. He had a very pompous voice, although this belied his character. He wanted to do some climbing and asked Rory and me if we would take him. We booked de Gasper and went to climb the Cinque Torre, the name given to five pinnacles of rock near Cortina, of which the Torre Inglese was a perpendicular thing about two to three hundred feet high. Half way up the Torre there was an overhang, and just below it, a piton on to which de Gasper belayed. Rory then followed, with Adrian next, followed by me at the end. De Gasper went over the overhang and told Rory to follow, but when it was Adrian's turn on the overhang, he fell off. The rope round his middle held him, so that his feet and his arms were roughly about the same level and he was suspended over about a hundred feet of nothing, revolving rather slowly, so he started becoming pompous.

I was absolutely killing myself with laughter so he gave me a bollocking and said stop laughing and bloody well get me down from here. The only way I could help him was to kick him, lean out and boot him out so I could catch him on the rebound. ... We had a good laugh about that incident and then actually took him on one or two other climbs, for he was fun.

CHAPTER FOUR

After the war and Rhodesia

In 1947 I was demobbed and started looking for something interesting to do. It was suggested I try the Wine Trade. My Great Uncle Iain, Grandad MacLeod's younger brother, had bought Mackintosh MacLeod & Co, a very old wine merchant based at Queen Mary's House, Inverness, overlooking the river. This beautiful old house has now been replaced with the horrible Highland Development Board's premises.

Uncle Angus proposed that I first spend six months in London with Smith & Hoey, a large wine business, learning how to manage a cellar. So I was given a room in my Aunt Joan's home, in Star House, on Chelsea Embankment. Peter Ustinov lived in the ground floor flat. He was fun and I remember he owned a huge old Mercedes.

I cannot say I learned a great deal at Smith & Hoey, except how to bottle and taste wine. I spent a lot of time attempting to copy the recipe for Pimms. Every time we got anywhere near the correct mixture, we were so drunk that we could not remember what we had put in.

It was during that period that I heard that my brother Alasdair had been killed in Palestine. He had originally joined the Scots Guards, but a silly squabble with me over seniority made him change his mind, so he transferred to the Cameron Highlanders with whom we had, of course, many family connections. He seems to have been attached to the Highland Light Infantry in Palestine, for some reason I do not know about. He was off duty one day, when he passed a brother officer clearing a cave of mines. He went to investigate and trod on a mine, which blew his legs off and blinded him.

There was no way in which he could have been mended, I understand. As the tremendous athlete that he was, it was probably better for him that he did not survive.

My brother Alasdair about 1947

He had had a great love affair with Daphne Oldham, who subsequently married Billy Hugonin, the Northumberland Estate factor and great friend of mine at Eton. Had Alasdair survived, I am sure he would have had a very colourful life, for he was very good looking and made friends easily. His death was a dreadful and irreplaceable loss to both my parents, and to us all.

***

Moniack Castle by Inverness, the home of the Fraser family and Innes House by Elgin where Iain and Margeret Tennant dispensed hospitality, were my frequent weekend stamping grounds. Rory Fraser and I used to flight geese on the Beauly Firth in a couple of barrels sunk in the mud about 300 yards out from Lentran station. One evening by myself I had two or three birds just as the tide was coming in, so decided to wait just a little longer. In no time the tide had overtaken me and I had to swim back to shore, carrying a gun and the geese. It was an experience I would not like to repeat.

After six months at Smith & Hoey, I returned to Inverness to complete the planned year at Mackintosh MacLeod & Co. I had a room over the front door of Rannoch Lodge. That establishment is now Crown Court where the Scots Guards Association dinner is held, so that always brings back memories.

There was quite a lot of really old wine in the cellars at Queen Mary's house, head office of Mackintosh MacLeod & Co. It had never been fully looked at. Fresh from London with all my new ideas, I told the manager the first thing we must do is go through all the stocks. This we did, but you couldn't see what there was as there were no labels, or they were illegible. The corks had gone on quite a lot of them so I said it was a waste of time doing the stock take there. It would be much better if we shipped the whole lot over to Skye where we could go through it all and see what we had.

Like a bloody fool, he agreed. So I bundled it all up and brought it to Tayinloan. Then we went through it. Most of it was hopeless and too far gone. But there were two bottles of 1898 Chateau Lafitte which were absolutely priceless, and they were all right. We decanted one bottle into my father's best decanter... and I knocked it over so we broke the best decanter and also lost the wine. That really was a disaster.

After that I realised that I was going to become an alcoholic if I kept this up, and it was also a realisation that you can't just sit there and wait for dead men. Or at least, I could not. So I resigned.

I was much criticised by my mother for giving up this wonderful opportunity, and I suppose a lot of people thought it was quite silly. But I don't regret having done it at all. And later exactly the same thing happened with the White Heather Laundry. Another opportunity fell into my lap, or so they thought, and I gave that up too.

After six months in Inverness I was living on practically nothing, with no capital or anything. I was in love with Philippa Guise, with whom I had been to all the various Balls in the Highlands. Rory Fraser had brought her to Skye for the Balls in 1947, but I took her over from him. I thought she was rather splendid, very good looking, and seemed to like my ideas. We went to a number of Balls together that year, I think it was 17 dances in 21 days, each one finishing in the early hours. How we managed the driving, I am really not too sure.

Rory Fraser had decided to head for Southern Rhodesia, where his mother's family, the Grimstons, had The Forrester Estate with five or six sections all growing tobacco. I thought I would try my luck there and emigrate too.

I went to see Bullard King & Company, which was based in London, to ask if I could work my passage to Rhodesia. At that time, I had a bowler hat and a folding Corgi motor scooter - designed for airborne forces, parachuting, or at least, that was the theory. It was quite uncomfortable, so I went to a scrap yard and got the front seat of a Daimler and put it on instead of the saddle. It looked a bit strange but it was very comfortable, although a bit unstable.

Riding this contraption on my way to the city offices of Bullard King, I went via St James's Street (which at that time was a two-way street and made of wooden blocks). It was rather wet and very slippery and I failed to make the corner at the bottom. I skidded across the road in my bowler hat, landing up underneath the sentry outside St James' Palace. It turned out that he had been a guardsman in my platoon and was not quite sure whether to salute or to roar with laughter; so he did both and said "oh it's you Sir!".

Mr Harvey, the clerk behind the desk at Bullard King & Company, did not bat an eyelid when I walked in with the bowler hat and an umbrella under my arm. I told him I would like a job please, as an ocean labourer. He asked me a very few questions, fished out some papers and signed me on, at a shilling a month, to go to Cape Town. I was to be the assistant cattleman on a cattle boat, the SS Umtata.

The SS Umtata was about 10,000 tons and had six passengers booked. They were travelling to work on the Rhodesian railways and had paid their own fares. There were also 25 Pedigree Angus bulls, two Herefords and two horses. The head cattleman was a Mr Kevin Lenahan, who Mr Harvey told me I must meet and make my own arrangements with him to board in time for sailing.

I was not quite sure what to do. At that time I was staying in the dormitory of the Guards Club in Charles Street. The hall porter was Gordon, who was a great ally and well used to covering up for anything that did sometimes occur there.

So I arranged for Kevin Lenahan, this renegade head cattleman fellow, to come and meet me in the Guards Club. It was not a very clever idea of course, because he wasn't really the right sort of character to introduce to the Guards Club. Gordon let him in and he started to behave as if he was in a pub or somewhere of the sort. This created a terrible scene and Gordon tried to throw him out. When I appeared I said he was my friend, which took a bit of laughing off. I got a frightful rocket from the authorities for bringing such disreputable people into the Club. He was a wild Irish boxer, who knew which end of the cattle to put the food in and that was about all. I could see that he had a great twinkle and a laugh, and we instantly made friends. But he was as wild as hell and good fun.

We arranged to meet on the ship, in the London docks, at a certain time. The crew were Indian Lascar seamen, led by a very aggressive British fellow who immediately tried to bully me into joining the trades union. I said balls to that and we practically had a fight. Kevin came to my rescue and backed me up, as he wasn't interested in the union either, but in this way, it turned out, we established our position.

After we'd been at sea for a few days we realised that the six passengers, young men who were going to work on the Rhodesian railways, were bored stiff. Because we had to feed the cattle and muck them out, it occurred to me that they might want something to do. So we lined them up and said "right! We could do with some help, so what about learning about cattle? You can do the watering and the feeding". They loved it; so Kevin and I just lay in the hay, directing them. As it got closer to the warmer climates, it was rather pleasant and so we actually had a wonderful passage.

All went well until we got to Las Palmas. The Captain said that either Kevin or I could go ashore, but one of us had to stay on board to look after the cattle. So we split the boys into two parties, and Kevin sent me ashore first with two or three of the lads. We looked around the island, had a drink, and came back. Then Kevin left, saying he would be back at four o'clock with the rest of his team.

At four o'clock there was no sign of him, whereupon the Captain started to get a bit agitated. Then a disturbance occurred at the far end of the pier and I saw a lot of people surrounding this fellow who was fighting drunk. The boys, it turned out, were trying to get Kevin to come back. They manhandled him back on board in a fighting mood, lashing out all over the place, and the Captain told me to get him down below and lock him in his bunk. I thought I had shut him in properly, so I set off to water the cattle and do the evening run.

When I got to the horses, one of them was making the most frightful noise. It was squealing and hammering away at the door and making a terrible fuss. I opened the door, to see what on earth was going on, and there was Kevin, trying to fight it. The horse was up on its hind legs and Kevin was fighting with his fists and was covered with blood and bruises. I think he'd set out with the intention of feeding the horse, but the horse, understandably hadn't taken to him. So we all set out for the Cape, slightly the worse for wear.

But it was a beautiful passage, with flying fish, whales, dolphins and the odd albatross. I ate my very first avocado on board, for the Lascar crew provided our food. I had no idea what to do with an avocado, which I found absolutely disgusting, having put sugar on it.

Cape Town's red light area was called District 6. It was out of bounds to whites, but Kevin thought he would try it out. I had a demob tweed jacket that a grateful army had given me when I left, so he borrowed it and set off. In no time at all there was a radio call to the Captain saying could we come and collect this corpse. Kevin had found some trouble somewhere and was carted off to hospital. I did get my jacket back, but absolutely stiff with blood, and we had to leave Kevin in the hospital and sadly that was the last I ever saw of him. I was intending to go on to Rhodesia from there, but the Captain asked me to take the cattle on to Durban, via Port Elizabeth and East London, and relieve Kevin as head cattleman.

The owners of the Angus bulls came on board in Durban. They were impressed with the way they were looking - thanks to all these boys who'd done all the work. I collected two or three hundred quid in tips, as of course poor old Kevin wasn't there. Finally I got off in Durban and the owners sent me back to Cape Town on the Blue Train, which was very luxurious.

I went to stay with friends of Uncle Angus, Max and Fay Maskell. They had a lovely house, The Old Brewery in Constantia. They owned the Bertram's Winery business in Cape Town. While I was there I met May Moray, the Countess, and her son Douglas, later to become The Bonny Earl of Moray, at Darnaway. Douglas had a great friend whose name I forget, but he taught me to fly again while there. Although I had had some experience at Eton, I never actually went solo. We had a lot of fun doing that. The house was extremely comfortable and a colossal contrast to my previous time as a cattleman. It also made me feel rather uncomfortable and restless though, so I set out for Rhodesia.

Arriving at the Rhodesian frontier I was surprised to discover that, without any employment arranged, I was not going to be allowed in to the country. Very quickly, and making an excuse, I found a telephone directory. I saw 'Harrison & Hughson' in large type, described as agents and so I told the authorities I had a job with them. That meant that I had to get round there pretty quick and sell myself, which I managed to do, but the job was selling knives, forks and spoons. I managed to get the sack fairly soon, but the job had served its purpose. I was in Rhodesia.

The next challenge was to get a more suitable job. I had no introductions so found a cattle ranch, the Glenara Estate, not too far from Salisbury. I asked if they would employ me in view of my cattleman's job on the boat and they took me on. The manager, Calmeyer, was an unpleasant South African fellow. I drove a huge tractor and one day I thought I had struck oil or something because a liquid started to leak out of one of the wheels. I had run over a sharp spike that had torn the tyre, which was in turn, filled with water to add stability, but it was a big surprise to me.

One night, after Calmeyer had been a particular nuisance, a huge great Pole who was also working with me, and I decided that we had had enough. We put a donkey into Calmeyer's bedroom. It climbed up onto his bed and crapped down the wall. When this was discovered, my Polish friend and I were told to clear it up. We both decided to tell him to do it himself, in suitable language, and departed the Glenara Estate in a hurry.

I must have saved a little money by then because I bought an old Chevrolet Coup Imp, which was a 2-seater truck. I set out in the truck to explore the River Zambezi, driving a long way through the bush to just below the Victoria Falls at Livingstone. It had occurred to me that we might be able to make some money out of crocodile skins and a trip down the river would help discover if the idea was feasible.

The plan was to arrange for some "boys" as the natives were then often called, to take me downstream in a canoe. I had heard that salt was a good currency so in my best Swahili - which was very basic indeed - I thought I had fixed the trip. I returned to civilization to contact Rory Fraser, who was staying in Kenya with John Bevan before arriving in Salisbury. I sent him a cable, telling of my plans and the immediate reply came back: "Arriving tomorrow, Rory".

I had met Mick Brassey somewhere on my travels. He was surveying the area for the planned Kariba Dam, about 300 miles downstream from the Falls. We arranged to visit him on our journey down the river and he agreed to hang a rubber tyre onto a tree overlooking the river, so that we would know when we had reached his camp.

Croc shooting on the Zambezi 1948

I had a .45 Colt pistol and Rory bought a .303 rifle. We gathered supplies; put a 40 gallon tin of petrol in the back of the truck and set off for the river. About half way there, perhaps 30 miles or so into the bush, the universal joint on the drive shaft broke. There we were on a disused track with no prospect of rescue, when to our complete surprise a truck, which only normally headed that way once a year, loomed into view.

Rory and I had decided that we should finish the whisky first and then see what could be done, but this sudden unexpected arrival enabled us to commandeer a lift in the truck to the river, where I had earlier organised a team to be waiting for us. Full of the spirit of enterprise and adventure, we set off in a dugout canoe with two boys each fore and aft, while Rory and I sat in the middle, absolutely delighted with our start.

After we had covered around 20 miles we set up camp in a splendid spot, tremendously pleased with ourselves. We slept well, in spite of many jungle noises that we had not experienced before.

Waking, full of anticipation, in the morning, there was no sign of our boys. They had buggered off in the night, having completely misunderstood our intentions of carrying on for much longer. Retreat was clearly impossible so, in a slightly disenchanted atmosphere, we set off on foot to the next village. There we were able to persuade another native crew to carry us on. So it went on like that with several different crews. We were able to pay our way with game that we shot between trips. It was very peaceful on the river except when we came to rapids. Then we would probably just have to skirt round them or in some rather fun times, dare to shoot them.

One was always conscious of the crocodile threats and tiger fish, which had a fearsome reputation, but the most interesting times were when we came across herds of hippos, half submerged and occasionally making rather threatening noises. I used to fire a shot or two into the water to deter an approaching hippo, but never actually aimed at one.

I was completely unaware that later on, five dead hippos had floated under the bridge at Kariba, nor that a policeman had been dispatched to find and arrest the perpetrators.

We eventually reached Mick Brassey's camp, and I regret to report that we were celebrating suitably when the policeman arrived to enquire "who dunnit". Naturally we denied all knowledge of such a crime. Then we threw him in the river and scarpered.

Years later, Jamie Guise, Philippa's brother, had a wedding anniversary party in The Turf Club in London, to which I was invited. There were a whole lot of people there, including a man with very white hair sitting quite close to Jamie, who'd also spent time in Rhodesia. He looked at me... and I looked at him... and this was the bloody policeman who'd landed in the river, fifty years earlier. I told him he couldn't arrest me now, and he said he was no longer a policeman and we had a very good laugh about it.

Apart from the hippos, we could pretty much shoot what we wanted. One night on the river the locals came to us to complain about a particular rogue elephant, which was causing a lot of trouble. They asked if we'd shoot it. The local commissioner's son also heard about it. He actually shot it, but it charged after he fired and landed about two feet away from us. It was huge and very exciting to be there at the time, but I don't think I would have wanted to shoot one myself.

After our trip down the river we had a bit of a party in Meikle's Hotel in Salisbury, which ended with Rory chasing me into the attic with a fire extinguisher that was actually going off. I think I took another extinguisher to fire back, and there we were in the attic spraying each other when the floor gave way. We fell through the ceiling and ended up in the bedroom below where there was a man in bed wearing green silk pyjamas.

We landed on the end of his bed, embroiled with each other, still fighting, in a pile of plaster. We carried on fighting and he woke up and wasn't at all pleased. I will never forget the look on his face as he woke up. We were blacklisted from the hotel after that and presented with a very big bill.

The plan to sell crocodile skins was cooked up mainly to pay for the trip, but it gave me a very good idea of what the country was about. Who were the enterprising people, what they were doing and what you could do. We had half a dozen skins that we had shot en route and we sold them for £5 each in Livingstone. When I got home though, I went to see Algy Asprey, a former motorbike instructor in the Scots Guards and member of the family of jewellers, to ask him what he would have paid for the skins. £1 a square inch was his reply, as my skins were around 360 square inches, I don't think we made quite the best bargain in Livingstone.

There was a lot of grant aid available to Rhodesian ex-servicemen at that time, but of course that wasn't for us. Rory had his plans and said he wasn't going to come back to London until he'd made a million. Sadly he didn't manage that, poor old thing.

He stayed on in Rhodesia and bought a farm with Mark Gaysford. He married Mary Drage, the famous ballerina, and produced a splendid family there but the climate was wrong for him in Rhodesia, so he eventually came back to the UK. He got very bad asthma, which eventually killed him.

He was a great man and a huge amount of fun. He was a huge enthusiast who would do anything you'd suggest to him and it would always be fun when you did it with him. He was a wonderful companion and a huge laugh.

After the crocodile trip I went to Salisbury (now Harare) to work as a labourer for Pop Caldicott, then Rhodesia's Minister for Agriculture. An early settler, he was a big man and a tobacco farmer. I ploughed and planted the seedbeds on his home farm. They had to be covered with vermiculite to retain moisture.

During this time, I heard of Philippa Guise's engagement to Rory's brother, Sandy Fraser. I decided to return home and put a stop to it. I do not think I would have come back otherwise. On the pier at Cape Town, just getting ready to embark on my return passage, I found the whaling ship, Balena, preparing to leave. I thought I should really be much better to have a go at that. I approached them and was offered a job as a gunner's mate.

I tossed a coin and it came up heads, so home it was.

But having got back to London, I decided I'd better stay. Which was silly, really. I liked the people in Rhodesia and there was a great feeling of enterprise. It was all very colonial with quite a lot of hard drinking, but the climate was lovely and it is a very beautiful country. The whites were adventurous, hospitable, hard people and seemed to have a good working relationship with the black population. There was no question of equality at that time. But the uncomfortable feeling you had in South Africa because of apartheid, didn't apply in Rhodesia. There was segregation but no strict apartheid.

You could certainly see the writing on the wall in South Africa, but not in Rhodesia. I subsequently found Kenya a very nice place and think if I'd gone there, I might have been tempted to stay there. It had all been a good contrast to life as a young Brigade of Guards officer.

There were two particular people I remember from that period, both of whom heard of my comings and goings in the country, and were sympathetic. Tony Coombe had killed a lion with his gralloching knife as it was eating his leg off; and Angus Graham - as he called himself. Angus was actually the Duke of Montrose, a member of Ian Smith's government, where he had made a name for himself. He offered me hospitality when he heard about the Calmeyer and the donkey incident.

Back in London, it became obvious that Philippa was going to convert to Catholicism, under Sandy's family influence. She had developed appendicitis and been incarcerated in a Catholic hospital somewhere. I set out to challenge the situation, laden with expensive gifts of grapes etc. when Sandy appeared with a box of dates, half of which he had eaten on the bus, on the way there. I thought that if he had that level of confidence it was time to give up after that. He and I had not completed the duel with which I charged him to, probably I think because he made me laugh too much.

I was quite upset about Philippa's decision and thought that converting was quite wrong for her, but as I was only 22, I just got on with it. Her father, Sir Anslem was a strong ally of mine and did not like Catholics at all. Her mother, a lovely person, whose grandfather was the Grant, of Speke and Grant fame, who discovered the source of the Nile. She tolerated whatever was going to happen.

Rather reluctantly, I then signed up to work for my father's brother, Uncle Rocky at the White Heather Laundry. It was not a very suitable job for me really, but I was persuaded to try it because of the family interest. My mother was convinced that as the eldest grandson, it would all fall into my lap. But I was not cut out to be a successful laundryman.

I was staying with Aunt Joan in London at that time. Her brother-in-law, Uncle Angus, was an alcoholic, although not openly called one. The condition was well known - certainly in my family. He did booze too much but he was very funny with it, and also very generous.

One morning, at about four o'clock, Uncle Angus appeared at the end of my bed with two bottles of champagne. He said: 'come on Ruaraidh, wake up!' I said 'no, no, I want to go back to sleep', but he said, 'come on, wake up, have a glass'. By this time, he was in fairly good order, so I agreed. After one glass of champagne at four o'clock in the morning, I was awake. The two bottles seemed to disappear, and then we were both in pretty good order.

Uncle Angus suggested we went to Covent Garden. So off we went and he bought every single potted plant that came up for auction. We got hundreds of these bloody things. By this time it was about six o'clock, so he said, "Right, you've got lots of girlfriends, let's deliver all these potted plants to them". But strangely enough no one wanted to see us with a potted plant at six o'clock in the morning in a somewhat pickled state.

He was tremendous fun but died when he was only about forty, having founded the Shuttlecock Club in St Moritz. It remains a splendid tribute to his memory today. (To qualify for membership, the tie and to attend the annual dinner, you need to fall off the Cresta Run at Shuttlecock corner.)

My employment in the laundry came to a sticky end about the same time as I got engaged to Sheena Mackintosh. My mother-in-law to be, Lady Jean Bell, (then Zinovieff) met my father for the first time and said "How nice it is that Ruaraidh has a job in the family firm", to which he had to reply, "Well, I am afraid he was sacked this morning!"

I had apparently been walking round the top of the White Heather factory chimney for some reason that I forget, when all the women came out to watch, meanwhile the Queen's smalls were shrunk. I think sacking me was actually the best thing my uncle ever did, for I was not a good employee, particularly for him.

CHAPTER FIVE

The SAS

On my return from Rhodesia, I discovered that the SAS was in danger of being obliterated. Brian Franks, who had commanded 2 SAS in Europe, took over The Artists Rifles Regiment at Dukes Road, London and gathered some experienced former members of the wartime regiment as a nucleus. They were determined to prevent the authorities from winding up all the so-called "private armies" that had developed during the war and the SAS was one of their targets.

Fortunately Brian, with David Stirling's support, persuaded the authorities that the concept of the SAS was far too valuable an idea to be allowed to disappear, so they secured agreement to keep it alive, albeit as a territorial organisation, by taking over the Artists Rifles. So that period was actually a vitally important time for the Regiment, without which it might well not exist today.

In order to qualify to join The Artists Rifles I had to resign my commission in the Scots Guards and in 1950 I re-joined as a Trooper in B Squadron 21 SAS under the legendary Ian Lapraik. He had 2 DSO's and 3 MC's, which made him an interesting Commanding Officer and so that meant I became a territorial soldier, fitting in these activities around my other employment which I did with great enthusiasm for the next 17 years.

After about a year as a Trooper, in 1951 I was commissioned again and joined The Boat Troop under Ian Murfitt, an ex-naval officer, from whom I later took over command. We were using the Mark 1, 2-star canoe, which had flotation bags round the side and was almost completely unsinkable. We discovered its wonderful seaworthy qualities, which I remember well, on a night time circumnavigation of Anglesey, which had some very interesting tidal races around it.

In 1951 I was privileged to command the Guard of Honour for the annual opening of the Royal Academy by Winston Churchill. He inspected us on arrival, after which I had to move pretty quickly and change into blues so that I could then attend the dinner; and a very special occasion that was. We had to march from Dukes Road to The Royal Academy in Piccadilly.

Commanding Royal Academy Guard with Churchill

The Boat Troop did a number of exercises with HMS Dolphin, the submarine base at Portsmouth, and I particularly valued the navigation instruction from Ian Murfitt, who had extensive naval experience.

My parachute course at Ringway was great fun. I remember when it came to my first balloon jump, the dispatcher was expected to give you a bang on the back to get you going when the "Green On" light came up. I was probably a bit full of myself until that point, because when it came to my turn, he just whispered in my ear "OK, Hilleary, you go when you want to!!"

Bloody hell that made it SO much more difficult! I had greatly enjoyed all the ground training and was very fit, so perhaps the dispatcher did not think I was scared. Little did he know! I think I was number five in that stick, but I must have jumped fairly swiftly, because I overtook Nick Day on the way down on account of the fact that he was very small.

Peter Wright was the transport officer in 21 SAS and decided on one occasion that we should get a Land Rover on to the top of Snowdon, which involved some pretty stiff handling - it needed to be carried part of the way up. He also wanted to demonstrate how to float a Land Rover across Frensham Ponds on the canvas canopy of a 3-ton lorry. It worked the first time, but unfortunately a second attempt did not. We sank the Land Rover.

Brian Whiting was the padre for 21 SAS who had boxed at Oxford, been a Baptist Minister before converting back to the Church of England where he invariably delivered the most compelling sermons, which I would have travelled many a mile to hear. We used to brawl together after dinner in the Officers Mess and so I had the greatest respect for his attitude towards the church generally. In his private life he was responsible for a parish in Devon and indeed married my daughter, Dhileas to Ben, as well as Alasdair and Fiona. But a drunken hippy appeared at his doorstep one Christmas time, demanding cash. When Brian refused him, the hippy took a swing at him which was not a good idea. Brian fired back, knocked the hippy's teeth out cutting his hand in the process. Both the hippy and Brian landed up in hospital together where Brian developed hepatitis, and died. Such a tragic waste.

There were various exercises in Norway, learning how to live in a snow hole and langlaufing at Kvamskogen near Bergen. There I made tremendous friends with Harald Risnes, who was the Colonel of Heimevernet, the local Regiment of the Bergen area. He had been extensively decorated working with Special Operations Executive (SOE), the Linge Company and the Shetland Bus during the war.

He had married his wife, Aslaug, on a glacier while on the run from a German prison. Aslaug had been captured after running a major part of the underground in Bergen. Harald and Bjorn Vest, the code name for the local underground organisation, had broken her out of the prison, for she had much information that could not have been divulged to the hated German occupation.

I subsequently returned to Bergen with Sheena to spend an amazing fortnight cruising round the Hardanger Fjord with Harald and Aslaug on his so-called "military boat", which was actually a very comfortable converted fishing boat. It had a six-pounder gun mounted on the bow, to make it look military, but otherwise was really a most comfortable yacht. We were given an unforgettable reception at every single port of call all around the Fjord for Harald was extremely well known everywhere for his wartime record. I do not remember being sober for a moment during the whole of that trip.

On another occasion Harald telephoned me in Scotland, from Norway, and ordered me to attend a drinks party on board a Norwegian destroyer in Loch Ewe. I told him that this was the other side of Scotland from Sanquhar, where we were living at the time but he would hear of no objections, so we went.

By coincidence, when we arrived at Loch Ewe we found the Eton Corps camped on the shore, but no obvious means of reaching the Norwegian destroyer, so I commandeered a canoe from them and set out (in a kilt and with Sheena on board) to be greeted right royally. On hiccupping our way off some hours later, I said rather rashly "You must all come to lunch tomorrow", little thinking that that would be possible.

But the following day, just before lunch, 40 Norwegian soldiers arrived in a bus. We rushed to arrange food supplies and managed to snaffle every haggis in Forres, plus the whole of my drink supply, which was then just about able to satisfy what became a very funny party indeed. The following year they did it again, but slightly nearer home at Montrose, and a wonderful range of friends was established.

When I later represented the Regiment at Harald's funeral, Aslaug gave me a copy of the wartime record of Bjorn Vest, and what a proud record that is.

I always wonder if we would have taken to the hills to defend our country as the Norwegians did, even though they knew their families would be taken out and shot if they were caught.

On another exercise, in the south of Germany, when David Sutherland was commanding the Regiment, I volunteered to see if I could arrange to get us transported home by air with the Americans instead of going by rail. I went to see the Army Air Corps at Melun, who are known as "The Teeny Weeny Airways" in some quarters, and are an extremely helpful lot.

They flew me up to Fontainebleau where the UN Headquarters was based. On arrival at the very small airport, there was no transport available to take me to the main base, except the Air Marshall's car, which was parked nearby. The corporal in charge of the Control Tower refused to let me take it, so I suggested that he looked the other way while I helped myself. The car had a splendidly important looking flag inside which I put on the pole on the bonnet and set off. There were several check points en route, at which I simply pretended to be the Air Marshall. I managed to make it through to the Commander-in-Chief's office, where I was able to arrange for the required transport. I could not resist telephoning David Sutherland the news from that office. He was furious and gave me a bollocking, sort of, but was quite pleased with the result nevertheless. I had later to explain how it was that the Air Marshall's car had done so many miles without a work ticket and I was charged some money for the petrol used.

One year we did an Escape and Evasion exercise in which I got caught and locked up in Oxford jail. We made such a nuisance of ourselves that the prison guards turned the water jets on us. It was not a pleasant experience because it knocks all the wind out of you. I do not recommend it.

A really dreadful man called Squadron Leader Parker was in charge of SAS Resistance to Interrogation training. He had an absurdly twisted sense of humour which was valuable, but one had to learn how to stomach great discomfort and overcome it.

On one exercise in the north of Norway we were transported by American C 119's and dropped 40 miles off course, up the wrong fjord, when testing the security of Bodo airfield, the most Northerly NATO defensive unit, against the Russians. Having completed the task, my friend, Jim Johnson, later to become the colonel behind the 'War that Never Was' in Yemen, and I, went to pay a visit to the Lapps and had some hilarious drinking sessions in the process. They are a nomadic race, very hospitable and with the women's breasts hanging right down to the ground while seated cross-legged on the floor of their tent. You should never enquire of a Lapp how many reindeer he has, for it is like asking how much money he has in the bank.

Following our winter warfare training in Norway I gave instruction in snow-holing to various troopers. On one occasion skiing at Aviemore, Johnny Duckett, a brother officer, broke his leg. He tells me that he only got a sleeper south after I had threatened to disconnect a carriage if he did not get a sleeper immediately - and it worked.

In 1960 I moved my family to Morayshire so was invited to take command of D Squadron 23 SAS at Invergowrie, near Dundee. The Squadron consisted of certain individuals from 15 Para whom I had to convert. It was the first SAS unit in Scotland and a cause for which I had long lobbied.

When that task was finished in 1967, it was the end of my 17 years with 21 and 23 SAS, both of which Regiments today are active and extremely efficient outfits. I am quite sure they are maintaining the proud traditions of the Originals. Today's boys are a great deal more effective than we ever were; but their "attitude" remains as ever, inimitable.

The regiment today has so many new commitments that were never envisaged in the early days, but the "attitude" of that bit extra, runs right through everybody involved today. I am very proud to have had a small part to play in preserving something that would have been disbanded had Brian Franks not stuck his neck out. Old fashioned thinking at the time would have had SAS disbanded and it would have all been lost. But I know that David Stirling's inspiration in the desert will keep something alive that has great significance today, as many current events continue to demonstrate.

CHAPTER SIX

Family

My very first girlfriend, when I was 15 or 16, wrote me a scented letter with hearts on it which was then passed round the dining room table at Skeabost one evening, to my hugely serious embarrassment. She was actually rather nice but I seemed to be a figure of fun then, and I did not enjoy that at all.

I had had one term of peace at Eton before war was declared, in September 1939. Practically my whole time there was spent with the war in the background. When I left school to join the Scots Guards in May 1944, Kipling's 'brutal and licentious' soldiery set the pace. It became possible to try the subject of sex out a bit more effectively in London, for my mother had suggested that it could be arranged for a price - as she somewhat awkwardly attempted to raise the subject. Of course, I had already heard much about the theory, but was pretty ignorant really...

When I arrived in Cologne with the 3rd Battalion Scots Guards, just after the war had ended, it became possible to visit Brussels on leave. At 71, Rue Prince Royale, there were some really lovely girls and one could practice everything one had ever envisaged. That was fun and at last sex came into a new perspective.

I met one of my first girlfriends in Italy. I was with the 1st Bn. Scots Guards in Trieste and I unexpectedly passed out one day while swimming. I had become more or less unconscious from a swelling in my throat and neck.

I was sent to hospital in Mestre where every morning I was immersed in a cold bath while the doctors watched me pass out again. Scratching their heads, they sent me back to bed to await another ducking the next day, with similar results. After several days of this rather tiresome treatment, I realised that I could walk out when I recovered, so I would set out for Venice each day. Exploring the beach on the Lido one day, I spotted a very attractive girl, Anne Delamain, with whom I developed a fun relationship. It continued for some time, until we broke up and she married Christopher Curtis, a very old friend from Eton.

The next girlfriend was Jane Chichester, who subsequently married another Scots Guards officer after I very stupidly rejected her advances. She would have been fun and an excellent wife I suspect, but Digby Hamilton was therefore to discover what I had lost. She was lovely and I think I made a mistake there!

I had quite a big thing with Jane Whitelaw, widely known as Blondie. She was a tremendous character, as was her father Grimy. But she had her eye on Laurence Rook, a glamorous Olympic horseman. She did eventually marry him, but sadly they never managed to have any children. This must have been a great disappointment, for she would have been a wonderful mother. She remains a very old friend and I still see her from time to time. Laurence subsequently died and she now lives in the lovely old castle in Gloucestershire with a fantastic shoot that I always used to enjoy enormously.

At that time there was an unwritten rule for so called "nice" girls, not to leap into bed very easily, or at all. Indeed, there was very little opportunity ever to try. It was extremely frustrating for a red-blooded fellow. One was expected to be married before sex became acceptable. That fitted with my desire to be married and have children while I was young enough to enjoy their company.

Dear old Alasdair Fraser of Moniack, my great friend Rory's father, was a fine example of a wonderful adventurous father figure with whom we had so much in common. He could not join in physically, as equals, although he certainly did so in spirit, even managing to escape from his wife to do so, occasionally.

I wanted to marry and have children when young. I could see that it was a lot of fun to be grown up because I had enjoyed my youth with older people, but I wanted to be friends with my children and to do things with them.

Before I left for Rhodesia in 1947, I had thought I was engaged to Philippa Guise. I had intended to create a bit of a nest and then bring her out to join me. I thought I would become a tobacco farmer and she would come out after I'd got myself organised, and we would farm. But that was not to be.

One year, I remember taking Brenda Gibbs and Jenny Ryder up to Skye in my 3 litre Bentley. It was when I was chasing after Sheena Mackintosh, who did become my wife. We set off from London at about six o'clock at night with a view to driving through the night and arriving at Tayinloan in the morning but the Bentley's lights kept going out. I could not work out why, so I mended the fuse a couple of times and eventually I got fed up and put a nail in. That worked beautifully for a bit until the car caught fire with smoke pouring from underneath the bonnet into where we were sitting. I had to pull all the wires from underneath the dashboard and disconnect everything to put the fire out and was then left on the roadside in the dark, with two girls in the back, and not much future.

A police car appeared, saw the trouble we were in and offered to get me to the Ram Jam Inn, up the road on the A1 where he said there was a garage that might be prepared to have a look at it. This policeman was a "great friend" of the Bentley Drivers Club, so he helped me find the right wires to make the car work, but we still didn't have any lights.

The policeman set off at 70 mph and I had to follow him. Sitting on his tail with no lights at all, flat out, was quite hairy. Anyway we finally got to the Ram Jam Inn and they reconnected everything and found the trouble, and off we set again.

At about six o'clock the next morning I was stopped for speeding as we entered Fort William. Then when I finally arrived at Tayinloan, I intended to stop in front of the garage doors, which faced onto the road, but I misjudged it slightly and went right through the doors instead. When my father came down to greet us I was sitting in the car with two girls in the back and the doors lying on top of the car, which was not a very popular arrival.

The Bentley was good fun. The water jacket around the cylinder block had stainless steel plates on all four sides, but the rear plate was corroded. On one occasion I was taking some girls, including Anthea Fairfax-Ross, to play tennis but the back plate sprang a leak and screams indicated that a jet of hot water had gone up Anthea's skirt.

The Skye Balls always happened for two nights running in September and one year I took Rory Fraser, Billy McPherson and Jamie Dunbar-Nasmith. Rory produced Philippa Guise and I took Jane Whitelaw but I hated large parties and always wanted to have small parties with good friends.

I first met Sheena when she was organising a ski party which she had asked me to join. I asked if I could bring Philippa along, but that went down like a lead balloon and I remember Sheena being rather upset about that. She didn't think it was funny at all, so in the end we didn't go.

I believe I had met Sheena before, at one of the Balls, but things didn't start happening until quite a bit later. She was living at Little Benhams, in Sussex with her mother, Lady Jean, the eldest daughter of Alfred Douglas Hamilton, the 13th Duke of Hamilton, and her stepfather, Leo Zinovieff, and I, meanwhile, was living with Aunt Joan at Star House in Chelsea. Sheena was the eldest in her family and had a sister Vora and two brothers, Douglas and Charlach. All four of them eventually became Olympic skiers.

My mother would always recommend going for a girl with money as her priority, but I valued spirit and enterprise rather more – and Sheena certainly had plenty of that.

She wouldn't pay any attention to me to start with and I had quite a lot of trouble breaking down the barriers. She had an idiotic Canadian fellow called George T. Fulford III, who was in love with her, and also Philip Woolley, a very nice but ineffective fellow, who would just sit there gawping, was another strong contender, for she had quite a lot of admirers.

George T. Fulford had a huge American motorcar and lots of money. One day he wanted her to come home to find her room full of roses. So he went off to some shop and ordered lots of roses ... but when they arrived, they all turned out to be rose plants with no blooms at all!

Sheena was dashing and a very strong character, glamorous in looks, but much more glamorous in character. Her music and laughter, together with her skiing, were very appealing indeed. I think she thought that I was a bit of a nuisance to start with and it took some time to get her attention or to notice me at all.

I do not think I did go on a ski party with her before we got married, as she was tied up with the Olympics at the time. She was in the Ladies Olympic Ski Team for the 1948 Winter Games in St. Moritz, and then captain of the Ladies Team in the 1952 Games in Oslo.

Sheena's uncle, Douglas ("Douglo"), the 14th Duke of Hamilton, had been the first man to fly over Everest. He was known as The Boxing Marquis, partly because in his earlier years he had knocked out the doorman of The Northern Meeting when refused entry and had been banned from the event as a result. He married Lady Elisabeth Percy, sister of the Duke of Northumberland.

The entire family were intriguing. Sheena's father, Lady Jean's first husband, the legendary Christopher Mackintosh, had played rugby for Scotland on the wing in 1924 and had been an Olympic long jumper in the 1924 "Chariots of Fire" Olympics; a member of the 1937 World Champion British Bobsleigh team and was particularly known as a World Champion skier, whose name still resonates in the Downhill Only Ski Club and in the Ski Club of Great Britain today. He seemed a most interesting and amusing man.

Christopher Mackintosh's father had started the Berlitz School of Languages, possibly as a cover for his spying activities. As a result, Christopher had spent much of his early childhood in Wengen, in Switzerland where they lived and where he must have perfected his skill on skis. His mother, who was a Whistler, eventually lived in very straitened circumstances in Monte Carlo, looked after by his funny old sister, Kathleen, known as "Aunty K".

Christopher's father died early and so he was looked after by a guardian and went to a public school in Eastbourne.

He later went to Oxford which is where he met the Hamilton family. As a very good-looking, charismatic athlete, he was accepted into the circle and eventually married Lady Jean, the 13th Duke's eldest daughter. The Duke had been a great naval officer and was known as "the Pocket Hercules" because he had actually dived under a battleship for a bet and hurt himself quite badly, as a result of which, he was pretty well crippled for the rest of his life.

The Duchess of Hamilton, Jean's mother, was rumoured to have had an affair with Lord Fisher, Admiral of the Fleet at that time. Jean was the second eldest of seven children, one of her brothers, Lord David married Prunella Stack, the founder of The Women's League of Health and Beauty, but he was killed in the RAF during the war.

Her younger brother, Lord Nigel, or Geordie as he was known, revived the extinct title of Earl of Selkirk and later became a Knight of the Thistle. He had been very successful in the RAF during the war, was Lord in Waiting to George IV and then Queen Elizabeth and later became Paymaster General and Chancellor of the Duchy of Lancaster. As QC, he became First Lord of the Admiralty in 1957 and then High Commissioner of Singapore and Commissioner General for South East Asia until about 1963.

Another brother, Lord Malcolm, was MP for Inverness-shire. He had an arranged marriage to Lady Pamela Bowes Lyon, which did not work out. He then married an American, Natalie Scarritt, who had been "Miss Bundles for Britain" in the war. She dragged him off to America where she could be Lady Malcolm. He started ferrying aeroplanes over to customers abroad, to escape his wife, I always suspected.

On a trip across Africa in 1964 he crashed his plane into Mount Cameroon with his son Niall on board. His remains were eventually found, but his son's body was not.

Lady Margaret, Jean's younger sister, married Major Jimmy Drummond Hay. Margaret was very beautiful and great fun, although I always thought her completely unscrupulous. Then lastly, there was Lady Mairi, who died early. They were all very good looking and athletic. The Dukedom of Hamilton is the premier Dukedom of Scotland and a very old title and the family had many acres, including Hamilton Palace, at Hamilton, Scotland's largest private house (until the house was demolished in 1927 when coal mining undermined it). The Hamilton mausoleum lies beside the A74 today, at Hamilton, and it has an extraordinary echo in it.

***

By the time I met Christopher Mackintosh, he and Jean had divorced (which they did in 1946). Christopher had remarried another wealthy woman, Irene Mann Thompson with whom he had two children. At that time I remember he had an office in Half Moon Street in London with a suspiciously beautiful secretary and a Bentley – and he was buying scrap metal in Jakarta and selling it all over the world, while living with Irene in her house in Maidenhead.

The office in Half Moon Street was run by a disbarred solicitor called Nevill, who looked exactly like a toad with thick spectacles. I always thought that having him around must have earned Christopher a questionable reputation...

Christopher later split with Irene and shacked up with her stable girl, who was many, many years his junior, and had two children by her when he was about 65 years old.

Christopher was very entertaining, extremely good company, told very funny stories and although I never skied with him, I imagine that really would have been wonderful, for he had a tremendous reputation that way. But he always seemed to me to be unable to tell the difference between truth and fiction. He would tell me tales of things, which I knew absolutely not to be true. He would tell me to my face that black was white, and expect me to believe it. I would say - I don't believe you Christopher, but he'd carry on with it. Some of it may have been in fun, but he was extraordinary and often seemed to persuade himself that what he was saying was true, so increasingly to me, something about him was never quite right.

He claimed he owned the patent rights to the biro pen. Then there was a long story of how he'd been badly done by and hadn't been given the profits he was due and so on. But the fact was, he may have had something to do with it all, but he didn't seem to me to ever have tied things up properly. There would be a long story about how he should have had something or other due to him and he really expected you to believe him.

He had an acute brain though, was certainly no fool, a brilliant linguist, charming, good looking, athletic, everything you could want from a man. He did something undercover during the war, I believe, but I have never discovered what it was.

Sheena and her sister Vora, absolutely doted on him.

***

I can't honestly remember exactly where I proposed to Sheena, but we got engaged in Skye and afterwards, in great excitement, we drove south in my 4½ Litre Bentley HPA 246. It was full of gumboots and fishing rods and guns and dead grouse. On the A1 coming south a new Bentley passed me. I was already doing about 80 and didn't think that was on, so I put my foot down and was doing about 100, pretty well flat out, when there was a frightful bang inside the engine and the piston broke in half. The con-rod didn't go out through the block like it might have done, so the top of the piston ended up rammed up into the block. In those old Bentleys, the block and the head were all cast in one piece.

So this was quite a problem with half the piston stuffed up into the top of the cylinder. We limped to a halt and had to get to Boroughbridge where the AA would tow us to a garage. I had to leave the car there, so we got the train with all our junk and loose stuff. It was a dreadful journey down and a most unfortunate start to our engagement. The car was going to cost so much to repair that I just sold it to the garage, very sadly.

Sheena and me

In Skye I remember we had dinner at Dunvegan Castle with old Dame Flora MacLeod one night. Coming back on the old road we had to cross over the Fairy Bridge. We stopped the car on the hill leading down to the bridge and got out. There was a very strange chill feeling in the still air when suddenly the doors slammed shut of their own accord in an impossible way. The two front doors lay forward, and we were pointing down the hill as we got out to look for fairies, when first one door closed, then the other. We both felt it was time to get back in the car and move on, so even today, Fairy Bridge holds a mystery for us both.

Sheena and I were married on June 14th, 1952. We started out renting a cottage called Howells, opposite Little Benhams, her mother's attractive house near the small village of Rusper, West Sussex. Leo Zinovieff, Jean's second husband had died in a train crash just before we were married and Little Benhams then became rather too large for Jean, so we bought it from her, on fairly favourable terms. Jean then bought Howells, the cottage that we had been renting, and moved in there. So we did a swap and Little Benhams was then our base until we went north in 1960.

Little Benhams had eight bedrooms and was very comfortable. Set in about eight acres near Rusper, West Sussex. I suppose we must have looked very respectable in those days and the house would of course be worth an absolute fortune today.

It was clear that I should have some more or less respectable employment now that I was going to be married. My parents had a great old friend, Alastair Urquhart, who had a little broking firm, Robertson Urquhart & Co. at Lloyds. He said that if I went and worked for a big company called C E Heath & Co. I'd be able to take the thing on if I played my cards right, because there were no "gentlemen" in the company. They were one of the biggest brokerages, but there was no one of any calibre in it. Alastair was a very dapper old man, immaculately dressed, with a DSO from the First World War, and he used to say, to make money, all you had to do was to get someone to insure their motorcar with you every day of the year. If you could do that, you could make a lot of money. He said in C E Heath & Co, I couldn't fail to get to the top.

So I joined C E Heath & Co and it soon became evident that he was quite right about the calibre of people (although funnily enough, my great friend Tony Stevenson was working there at that time, but only on a distant basis).

The Directors of C E Heath & Co came to the conclusion that as I was about to marry the niece of the Duke of Hamilton, I was clearly a grand sort of chap who could be pushed up front. I could talk to all my friends and make them do their insurance with me. So I was used, or they tried to use me, as a sort of vehicle. It was quite good for a bit and it was at times fun, but eventually I couldn't take it. I didn't like being used as a commission agent. If I wanted to see my friends, it was because I wanted to see them, not because I wanted to get some business out of them. And it became horrible. You began to think about, wherever you were going, how much they were going to be worth.

I did this job for five years, which is what you had to do to become a working name as a Member of Lloyds, which at that time was an extremely profitable thing to do. In order to come in on the cheapest basis you would have to deposit £10,000, which of course I didn't have at the time. My mother had made some vague indications that she might find the money, but when the time came I decided I didn't want to do it.

While I was working at Lloyds, I was commuting to London in a bowler hat and an umbrella (albeit in a three-wheeler car I had found!). I would have to walk across London Bridge, and watch all these people doing exactly the same thing and I can remember studying the faces and thinking to myself - what the hell are you all thinking about? It was just what they were going to do that day, and what they were going to do when they got home. There was no feeling of enterprise about it at all and the whole thing seemed like a huge great sausage machine. I am quite glad I stuck the job as long as I did, because I began to understand a little bit about how the City works, and I certainly did have many friends there, but in the end it really wasn't for me.

I used to go to lunch in the Captain's Room at Lloyds, although I had no business to be there at all. But it was quite fun getting in. There was a friend of mine called John Green whose father, Toby Green, ran an extremely successful marine syndicate. John had had some problem, which had caused all his hair to fall out. He came in one day, literally as bald as a coot. He was a pretty hard character, and didn't seem to mind much about this. He went to sit down in a deep leather armchair, and opened the Times. I can't think what possessed me, but I suddenly thought it would be quite funny to set fire to his Times. And he never moved. He simply never moved. He just sat there with this flaming Times, and let it burn. And that's quite tricky, not to panic, not to throw it away, because it jolly well burns you. He didn't even accuse me of doing something dreadful, which, of course, completely ruined my fun. He just got up and walked away, taking absolutely no notice of me at all.

***

Around this time another plan had begun to form in my mind and this seemed to be the moment. So I took the plunge and formed Hilleary and Waddell, which we established to operate Self Service Bendix Launderettes in London. I had met Peter Waddell who was training the Ladies Olympic Ski Team and he had started the first Bendix Launderette with Graeme McLintock, in Putney. Washing machines were on the cusp of becoming widely available, but were still unaffordable to many households and it sounded like a good route towards self-employment, so we joined forces and developed a chain of Bendix shops.

A number of people, including Aunt Joan, thought this was a good idea, and asked us to manage a launderette for them. Aunt Joan's was called Skyewash. Naps Brinkman, a lovely man, had another. He was Sir Napoleon Brinkman who owned a good part of Soho, an immaculate Grenadier Guardsman with two DSOs. He'd been taken prisoner in the war and climbed out of the prison on a barbed wire rope that he'd made. To meet him, you'd never think in a million years he could climb out on a rope, let alone a barbed wire rope. We opened one for him in Soho, and I think we had a chain of seven or eight all together, operated on a franchise basis.

I had no financial training of any sort. I knew how to spend money, and so when it came in I tended to get rid of it as quickly as I could. The trouble with launderettes was that it was all cash, and you put it in your pocket. If I had had some training we could have made some proper money from building it up, because it was certainly a good business and it produced plenty of good cash income. But instead, I started getting itchy feet for Scotland.

Early in our married life, there was some financial stress, strangely enough, which has remained with me pretty much ever since. In an effort get some economical transport I had bought a three wheeled car. When you turned the wheel at right angles, you could literally go round in circles on its own axis.

Later on we had a little tiny Austin van. We had two children then and a nanny called Anne who was rather prim. We drove through the night to Scotland once, with Anne and the children in the back. Sheena was in the front, it must have been a bit of a squash.

We got to Loch Garry in the morning as dawn was coming up, I was feeling a bit weary having driven all night. I stopped the car in a layby quite quietly, thinking everyone was asleep, and stripped off and went in for a swim. When I got out, Anne had woken up and saw this naked figure emerging from the loch and was terribly shocked. I don't think she lasted much beyond that. That would have been when we were coming up for a fortnight in the summer holidays to stay at Tayinloan with my father.

The number of nannies we then got through was horrendous – 32 in all I think. They couldn't take the pace. Even Nanno came to us for a while to look after our children, but it didn't work unfortunately. How Nanno stuck it with us when we were children, I will never know.

***

Bull terriers are definitely the stupidest dogs of all time with absolutely no brains at all. Sheena had one called The Horsa when we were at Little Benhams and one day we went to see a film called The Planter's Wife, in which there was a fight between a mongoose and a snake. I thought the mongoose was absolutely splendid and that it would be rather fun to get one. I can't remember where I got it from. It might have been Harrods.

I arrived home with this thing. It was very inquisitive. It used to look into everything and really was great fun. But Horsa was a dirty old male and as he sat in front of the fireplace with his pink carrot sticking out, the mongoose, which we had named Sticky, gave it a nip and the poor old Horsa retired hurt. We called it Sticky after Ricki Tiki Tavi because it used to get into the honey pot and get itself covered in honey.

Sticky was fun. He used to get into the bed and you'd see this little hump running around the bed. He knew exactly where to go. We had chickens and he used to pinch an egg for himself out of the bucket. Then he'd roll it along the floor, find a wall, then flip it between his back legs against the wall to crack it.

Eventually, a friend of Sheena's family, Anthony Muspratt-Williams, known as Sprat, said he would keep Sticky when we went off skiing. What to do with a mongoose when we went away was actually a bit of a problem. Sprat lived in Wiltshire, and something went wrong with him when we were away, and he went into hospital. Or did he go and visit someone in an old folk's home? Either way, he landed up in an old folk's home with Sticky. There was somebody in bed who'd been bedridden for months. Sticky escaped. He got into the bedridden fellow's bed and suddenly the wretched man was no longer bedridden. Sticky flushed him out completely. He ran screaming out of the room.

One year at Little Benhams we tried to make money with a turkey farm. We bought a lot of turkeys. A fellow SAS officer called Peter Wright, who had helped us take a Land Rover to the top of Snowdon, came to help build the turkey house. We had hundreds of them. At Christmas time we had to kill them and sell them. We asked Alasdhair Bullough over to join our turkey shoot. We quickly discovered that when we fired a shot, the others would all stick their heads up to see what was going on. I can't remember exactly how we killed them all, but we sold the turkeys and made rather a lot of money.

***

About that time Jean gave me a bundle of papers to look at, because she said her family solicitors had been crooked in some way. My solicitor, another brother SAS officer, Robert McWatt of Payne Hicks Beach, looked through everything and pointed out that the last Duke of Hamilton, Jean's father, had settled one hundred thousand pounds on each of his six children. However, his solicitors had run off with all the money. So, the old Duke had accepted the loss and then put another hundred thousand down for each one of them, which in those days was a great deal of money. Robert's advice was that there was a case against the Duke's solicitors, but Jean refused to take it up.

Jean was not always an easy mother-in-law and an impossible housekeeper. Having grown up in the Ducal household, she hadn't acquired the slightest idea about how to run a house. She practiced a studied vagueness about simple matters and I always thought that much of her daily life was a bit of an act. But in fact, she had taken her four children off to Canada during the war and they all had to pretty well do everything for themselves there. So you knew perfectly well that she was actually extremely capable.

I have to say about Jean though, that when there was a real crisis, she would become very sensible and very practical. Her mother, the old Duchess, seemed to me to be a complete crank about health and food, and that came down to Jean, and also a little bit down to Sheena's sister, Vora too.

I think I probably admire and look for adventure and a sense of humour, as being the qualities that intrigue me in someone the most. Sheena was absolutely brimming with both, but I don't think Jean ever showed quite as much of that. She had clearly been a very brave horsewoman in her youth and like many of her family, she had been an active participant in many sports, but it was sometimes hard to see that in everyday life. I think taking your family off to Canada at the beginning of the war, was understandable, but as the invasion never happened, it must have been difficult to come back and be with people who had not left.

I suppose there was a certain sort of vulnerability about her act, but if you got her in a corner and wanted to talk about something serious, she really was good, and made a lot of sense. She was a good person to talk to and had all sorts of sensible ideas, but once she started thinking that people were listening to her, or thought she was funny, the act would appear again.

After her divorce from Christopher Mackintosh, Jean had married Leo Zinovieff, a White Russian engineer who had previously been married to a Russian princess called Sofka. Sofka had become a communist and drove a taxi in Paris.

Sofka wrote a book - Sofka - about the life of a Parisian taxi driver. I never met her, but if you ever meet their son Peter, you needed to tread carefully no doubt because there had been a very strange background there.

Leo was a nice man. His family had written the Zinovieff Letter, which might have sorted out a lot of the trouble when the Czar was killed. Leo was in a business partnership with Hector MacLeod, step-father to Jane, Tony Stevenson's wife. He had his feet on the ground, with no airs or graces. As far as I could see he was a straightforward, decent, honest man. When he married Jean, I think they were probably very happy and he would have been very good for Jean. I think he would have provided a stable set up for her and it would have been a good marriage. But he was very sadly killed in a train crash when commuting to work. They had not been married for very long.

Jean was a widow for quite a long time after that, and sort of pottered around. Then she found Vivian Bell, who many years earlier had been the first man ever to kiss her. Vivian, in the meantime, had married an Argentinean, and had farmed in the Argentine all his life. His first wife had died after having produced two children, a son, Michael, (who was known to us as "the Plumber"), and a daughter, who married a keeper in Perthshire.

Vivian was a Member of the Royal Company of Archers, a tremendous snob, always immaculate and spoke fluent Spanish. So it was strange that he managed to be taken for a ride so badly, when they built their dream house in Barranco Blanco, near Mijas, in Spain. A crooked German, Haupt, had persuaded local farmers that he would pay them after he had developed a huge and very beautiful valley, which of course, he developed but never paid for.

Vivian died at their home in Spain. Jean couldn't stay there by herself so we bought her home. Then we had to decide what to do about the house. I was a bit spare, I hadn't got what you'd call steady employment, while Jackie Shaw Stewart, her other son-in-law, was in steady employment and very upright. He insisted that the lawyers who had dealt with Jean's business, Lawrence Messer, should handle the whole thing.

However, it became evident that the house in Mijas was unsalable as the legal complications were impossible to unravel. A Swiss family who had made a lot of money out of one-armed bandits were very close neighbours there. They became great allies and eventually bought the house from us. He was a nice chap but as fly as a barrow-load of monkeys with a very pretty wife.

Vivian's son, "the Plumber" was very practical. He lived in the Isle of Man and had all sorts of ideas about how to get the furniture from the house in Spain back in a van. We then set about refurbishing the house. We could not sell it so we had to let it, which is how I came to be there. It was quite fun. Letting the house, and getting to know all the people down there. We tried unsuccessfully to sell the house for years. I eventually told Jacky that I would eat my hat if he could get one hundred thousand pounds for it. Unfortunately they eventually did manage to sell it for that much. So I had to eat my hat – and I did (actually, it was Dhileas's hat, the night before she married Harry).

We were lucky to sell. It was a white elephant and a huge problem. I always thought we should have accepted half the price in cash, years before. But Jacky Shaw Stewart was insistent that it had to be done legally, and I think everyone was very puzzled by that. Because in those days no one ever did anything legally there!

It was an incredible place. There was a town hall nearby, which had a map of the borough and area surrounding Mijas. And there was a note underneath this map saying - of the 42 urbanisations of Mijas, 10 are legal. In other words, anyone thinking of buying houses in this area... watch it. It was incredible. Nothing was legal.

Even the car Vivian and Jean owned was illegal. It was an Austin Princess 4 Litre R car with a Rolls Royce engine. They took it into Spain and when the licence ran out, they didn't get it renewed. So it was illegally in the country and the authorities eventually, after 20 years, decided there was going to be a euro 200 fine for keeping it there. They tried to give it away, but the people who got it gave it back, because they realised they were going to be fined.

So it was given to my son, Duncan who was just leaving school and he and his friend, Gus Ward, along with their two girlfriends went to Spain to pick it up and drive it home. On their way up the Sierra Nevada the brakes failed and they had to navigate their way back to Granada and then from Granada back to Malaga, which Duncan drove with no brakes at all. They parked it in the airport and Duncan tried to give the car away to the airport controller in exchange for an air ticket. Somehow he got the air ticket but the man decided he didn't want the car after all, so it was left brakeless in Malaga airport.

So David Shaw Stewart and I set out a month or two later with new parts to try and get it out of the country. We filled the boot with lemons, and when we got to the frontier, we both got out, and started giving lemons to everybody. The Customs people got very upset at the queue that started to form, and said: come on, go through - so we got out! I think they thought we were quite mad so told us to clear off.

When we got home, Duncan used the car until he gave it to a friend, Whispering Nick (Lumsden), a fellow Scots Guards officer, in exchange for a packet of cigarettes. I don't think we should have done that, really. It was a jolly good car. Whispering Nick gave the car to his father who repaired it and then used it for commuting for many years!

***

My Children

My daughter, Dhileas married Ben Sanders, son of very old friends, Polly Macdonald of Blarour and Terence Sanders. They had Archie and Iona just before Ben died very suddenly of a heart attack, while cutting trees on the River Swale where they lived, at Ellerton Abbey, in Yorkshire. He was only 33. I had always rather hoped that she would marry a grouse moor and sure enough, they had one at Ellerton. It was a huge shock and a great sadness when Ben died, not really having had time to know his children at all.

Dhileas continued bravely for 10 years as a widow after which she married Harry Lukas, whose family own a grouse moor so that, at least, my ambition for my daughter was satisfied! They had Kirsty and Alexander and live in the Borders at Drumelzier. Kirsty might become a scientist and Alexander is teaching skiing in Japan.

Archie, Dhileas's elder son, married Miranda Appleby and had twin girls Rose and Isla and then a son, Benedict, my first great grandchildren. Archie runs a recycling business in England and will prosper, I have no doubt, for they are a well-established family I feel sure.

Iona, who was completely impossible as a child, set off for New Zealand where she met Alasdair Bentley, known as "B", a very skilful joiner. They married in October 2014 and have a lovely house in the most beautiful loch side town of Wanaka in the South Island. She has a splendid job running the tremendous winter sports activities of New Zealand - and perhaps to go with her name (Iona Bentley) they even bought a Bentley T Saloon. Terrific – I approve!

After serving in the Scots Guards, my son, Alasdair set himself up as a caricaturist and artist, using the name "Loon". He has been extremely successful over many years now. He married Fiona Baillie, daughter of my great old friend Michael, Lord Burton, of Dochfour. They had Flora, Rosannagh and Geordie who are also really splendid grandchildren, of whom I am very proud.

Fiona's mother was Philippa Guise's greatest friend, but she had had an unhappy marriage to Michael, which eventually came unstuck. I suspect that event had probably had a detrimental effect upon her. She was intensely proud of, and happy over Fiona's marriage to Alasdair though, so it was a great sadness for me that after Sheena and I had parted company, Fiona took Sheena's side.

Fiona did come to stay with me at the Home Farm in Portree on their return from their two-year honeymoon, which was lovely; but later years were less complementary. Perhaps her subsequent brain tumour and death did create a bridge again before she died, but that was a dreadful sadness for the family all over again.

It was unfortunate I did not get on with Fiona in quite the same way as I would have liked for it was not always like that. She was clearly upset but would not come and tell me what was bothering her and what she found so difficult. I could see that it was causing trouble for them and sad that I could not help. Fiona eventually did not like coming to Skye, although she loved Shiel Lodge, which belonged to her father. I don't really understand what it is that did not seem to gel with me.

Alasdair was very torn for he obviously loved his wife, and it was a conflicting interest for him. Fiona enjoyed going to Sheena, but I seemed to put her hackles up. It was a problem, and a great shame, for I would have liked to be able to laugh with them.

I think she had had a somewhat unhappy home background, when her parents were having difficulties. I don't think they ever showed much love to their children or to each other and, much as I like him, Michael is a pretty volcanic figure.

Alasdair and Fiona's eldest daughter, Flora, now shows budding restaurateurs in India how to get started. Rosannagh their second daughter has become engaged to Nick Stratton, and lastly Geordie, has completed his finals at Oxford Brookes and is trying for the Army. An excellent piper, he has been busking his way through life very successfully so far and I await great news of his future progress, which I suspect will be good.

As a father, I have probably done pretty well everything wrong, but I did want to be friends with my children. I was conscious of wanting to get married young and consequently being able to do things with them. After five years as a widower, Alasdair remarried Charlotte Westbury, who had married an Irish baronet called Jamie first time round and then Lord Richard Westbury, both of which had come unstuck.

Duncan also served in the Scots Guards and then set up a media business, which was a great success. He married Sophie Dunne whose family are really good fun and delightful. Sophie was a nursing sister and did her District Nurse qualification at Dunvegan, while staying with me here in Skye before getting married, so I was able to get to know her and love her so much. Her mother is also absolutely delightful and an excellent example of what I imagine to be one to follow. They have Mairi, Eliza and Hector, all of whom were, or are still at Rugby where Martin, Sophie's father, is a governor as well as the Lord Lieutenant of Warwickshire. His brother, Thomas is Lord Lieutenant of Herefordshire, so their splendid old mother, Peggy was really chuffed with her two sons. Their sister, Philippa, was married to George, Earl Jellicoe, the famous SBS and SAS figure of wartime reputation, prominent politician and industrialist. He sadly died a few years ago after a terrific life.

I take the view that children can only improve. I think they start off perfectly ghastly. When all the mothers were drooling over these little slobbery things, I was running a mile. As they get older they get more and more fun. Archie and Iona, who are the two oldest ones now, are terrific. You can discuss anything you like with them. I took them skiing once and they were great company.

***

I was very fond of my father and my mother. I suppose I was more of a friend of my father than my mother. I think Ewan, my brother, was less independently minded, and liked to emulate them more. But he was a very good athlete and was far more of a success than me in that way. He did well in the fish business.

Both my brothers Alasdair and Ewan were great athletes, and each were Keeper of the Field and Keeper of Oppidan wall at Eton, doing all the conventional things rather well.

My youngest brother, Ewan had bought my share of Tayinloan after my father had died. I sold because we had just bought Logie farm and Sheena would not come to Skye as I wanted. So Ewan and Susie, his wife, attempted to run it for holiday lets, but could not make it work as their third house and offered it for sale a few years later.

By this time Sheena and I had parted and I was setting myself up in Skye. Ewan and Susie received an offer which I agreed to match, however Ewan - for whatever reason I shall never understand - thought I could not afford that, so he would not sell to me. Instead he accepted the other offer. I never forgave him for that as he really did not have any knowledge of my circumstances and this was our last family house on the Island.

***

I think Sheena and I have sorted things out now and we can be friends. We don't have quite the same view of life today, but we have been very happy together and we've done many fun things and produced an amazing family, which was a great deal to do with her. She was a wonderful mother. And although she wonders perhaps if we should ever have got together in the first place, I certainly would never regret having married her and would never want to give that impression. We did have our problems and I didn't enjoy everything we did together. I diverted many times, which was a mistake for which I am sorry; but that's history now and you can't change it. Had Sheena been able to see past those indiscretions, who knows if we might still be together today... I always thought it was very silly to divorce, which I still think achieved absolutely nothing.

Sheena convinced herself, encouraged by certain others, that my affair with Philippa was the last straw. Sheena kept saying that I should really have married Philippa in the first place and that I was eventually going to marry her. Repeated assurances to the contrary, along with my view that we simply could not afford to keep Logie Farm, met deaf ears and Sheena's blind refusal to recognise these things, lay behind a lot of our troubles.

Had Dhileas not come to the rescue and bought a large part of Logie Farm, I think we would eventually have just gone bust.

I always knew that I could make a go of Skye though, in spite of my father's doubts. Indeed I eventually did so. Had Sheena agreed to sell Logie and come with me, and had Ewan not let me down over the sale of Tayinloan, we might have retained our old family home *and* prospered as well. But that was not to be.

I will end this chapter with a family favourite, sung lustily by all:

Lament for Maclean of Ardgour

Wail loudly ye women, your coronach doleful
Lament him ye pipers, tread solemn and slow
Mown down like a flower is the Chief of Ardgour
And the hearts of his clansmen are weary with woe.
In peacetime he ruled like a Father amongst us,
Unconquered in fight was the blade that he bore,
But the chase was the glory and pride of his manhood
Strong Donald the Hunter, MacGillean Mhor.
Low down by yon burn that's half hidden with heather
He lurked like a lion in the lair he knew well
T'was there sobbed the red deer to feel his keen dagger
There pierced by his arrow the caillzie cock fell.
How oft when at 'een he would watch for the wild fowl
Like lightening his coracle sped from the shore,
But still and for aye as we cross the lone lochan
Is Donald the Hunter, MacGillean Mhor.
Once more let his war cry resound in the mountains,
Macdonalds shall hear it in 'eery Glencoe,
Its echoes shall float o'er the braes of Lochaber
Till Stewarts at Appin that slogan shall know.
And borne by the waters beyond the Loch Linnhe
Twixt Morven and Mull where the tide eddies roar.
MacGilleans shall hear it and mourn for their kinsman
For Donald the Hunter, MacGillean Mhor.
Then here let him rest in the lap of Sgurr Donald
The wind for his watcher, the mist for his shroud,

Where the green and the grey moss will weave their wild tartans
A covering meet for a Chieftain so proud.
And free as an eagle these rocks were his eyrie
And free as an eagle his spirit shall soar
O'er the crags and the corries that 'erst knew his footfall
Of Donald the Hunter, MacGillean Mhor.
(from Songs of the North)

All of us at Iona's wedding

CHAPTER SEVEN

To Sanquhar House, 1960

By the end of the 1950s I wanted to come back to Scotland and open a launderette in Edinburgh, although of course I really wanted to be in Skye. My father was very much against it, as Skye was depopulating after the war, but I thought I could change that and make things happen.

My father had bought Beaton's Garage, which ran the local bus service and should have been a really good business. He had also started The West Coast Building Company, all great local enterprises and saw all kinds of possibilities, but he had never actually had to change a wheel himself so was unable to make the businesses profitable.

My great friend William Gordon-Cumming had recently bought the Sanquhar estate, near Forres, from old Mrs Edward, who was the widow of Alec Edward, my grandfather's friend for whom I had supplied venison at Kinloch before the war. I think William paid sixty thousand pounds for 2,000 acres of land and forest, plus the big mansion house with its own walled garden.

In the first year he cut sixty thousand pounds in timber and so he was soon back to zero. It was a great purchase and he had moved very quickly to get it, so he offered Sanquhar House and part of the estate to me for a very low rent. He also warned us that he would eventually pull it down in order to develop a housing estate in the garden.

I was godfather to William's son Alastair, as a very old friend, and he had also become godfather to my son Duncan; so this seemed to be a splendid way to move north and start off with an exciting new base.

Sanquhar House was a fine Victorian mansion, set in many acres of garden, with landscaped grounds, including two lochs surrounded by spectacular rhododendrons, a large walled garden with extensive greenhouses and a fine stable block. With 53 rooms in all, the house was certainly substantial, although it was a bit of a Victorian horror to look at. There was a main hall, decorated with crossed swords up the walls, and a substantial staircase. It had some very grand rooms, including a ballroom, a double floor height conservatory, a billiards room, several sitting rooms and a good-sized dining room. Including what became the four flats which we created, it must have had 18 or 20 bedrooms. So suddenly we now had an exciting new family base and gave the impression of having pots of money, with enough space to have lots and lots of people to stay - which we did.

Sanquhar House 1953 (Photograph courtesy of Ray Mills)

*** * ***

So we sold Little Benhams and, in the winter of 1960, arrived at Sanquhar, which Sheena had actually not seen before we moved in. I suppose it was quite a bold move and particularly brave of Sheena. We arrived in a big Land Rover with snowdrifts reaching over the top of the car. There was a huge snowfall that winter and Duncan was a screaming baby so there we were setting up shop in Sanquhar House – with the world at our feet.

I intended to invest some of the proceeds of the sale of Little Benhams into a commercial venture which would hopefully provide income. William owned some land on the shore, beside the lighthouse, at Lossiemouth, including a place called Covesea (pronounced "Cow-Sea"). He was keen to see it developed. I could see the potential for the leisure market on that coast and had become interested in the possibilities for caravans, because you could extract a very high income per acre. So William and I did a deal: he provided the land and I invested in the development and so we started the Silver Sands Caravan Park. I invested my capital on the basis that a manager would run the park. More about that later, but the plan was that once the operation was set up, I would then use my time to buy and sell game.

Salmon & Game Services of Scotland

It became clear to me that if someone caught a salmon on the Spey, it was difficult to do anything with it. So I started to run a van up the river, offering to buy salmon from anyone who wanted to sell. Sometimes we would come back with really quite a big number and then I had to do something with them. I built a smokehouse for some, sold others and this all became Salmon and Game Services of Scotland Ltd.

When I went shooting somewhere, I would offer to buy the bag and the result was I had a business and an awful lot of fun. By this time I was of course still embroiled in 21 SAS in Scotland. The regimental sergeant major, Bob Bennet, one of the Originals, wanted to leave London and come to Scotland, so I put him in charge of the van and of course, in no time at all, he knew all the ghillies up the river and we had large numbers of lovely fresh salmon.

We had ice but no refrigeration, so we had to get the fish off to the market as quickly as possible. Some went to Paris by air and many went to London in boxes on the train.

Sheila de Rochambeau, a larger than life relation of Sheena's, gave me an introduction to Fauchon in Paris - the Fortnum & Mason of France and Europe's most expensive shop. Fauchon said they would only take five pound sides of smoked salmon, but they liked what I was supplying. A five-pound side, however, has to come from a twenty-pound fish, so getting them was not so easy. Eventually I found a chap up in the hills behind Inverness who had a railway carriage in a wood - the most insanitary thing you've ever seen - but he smoked salmon quite beautifully and that was what Fauchon used to buy. No EEC regulations would have stood a chance, but Fauchon lapped it up.

I could not guarantee a supply, but whenever I did have any, that was where they went.

One year, while dining with Iain and Margaret Tennant, Iain complained he was not making any money out of the salmon nets at Lossiemouth. He had rented the netting rights from the Crown on a five-year lease and I happened to know the reason why he was not making money. The foreman of the nets was an old Scots Guardsman from the first world war, Tom Henderson, who was a great character, but tricky.

I offered to take the nets off Iain for the remainder of the season, for two hundred quid - the rent that he paid the Crown. I told Tom I was going to be there every time he fished the nets to which his face fell a mile. But we soon became good friends.

I told Tom I wanted to kill the first fish we caught. A fly net has a long string of poles with a net, running out at right angles from the shore with a box of net at the end, supported on poles. To get at this box when the tide was out, we had to climb along a rope, strung along the top of the poles, like a monkey, landing up over the top of the box. We then opened a hole in the top of the net, and scooped out the fish with a landing net. The fish were then killed with a lump of wood called a priest. This is difficult to do while holding onto the rope with one hand and the landing net with the other, while holding the priest at the same time.

Tom said he would help me to kill the first fish, so we were both struggling away like this, and I took a swipe at the fish, and hit Tom on the leg. He let out a yell and grabbed me and we both fell into the net.

We also had a jumper net. This was a simpler contraption, with another line of net running out from the shore, but the box not quite so big as the fly net. The third kind of net was a sweep. There the net was put in a boat while we watched to see if the fish were going to run up the river. When they were just about to run, we rowed out and tried to encircle them with this net.

On one occasion we were watching when we saw the fish moving out to sea, ready to run. I said to Tom: "I think they're ready to go now." He said: "No, wait, they're not ready yet." After a bit of an argument I said: "Look, I'm paying the rent, we're bloody well going when I say we're going, and we're going now."

So we shot the net and we got 750 salmon in the net. It was heaving with fish. We got the whole shoal. But the net burst and all the unemployed characters in Lossiemouth were sitting on the pier watching, and they all disappeared off the pier and came down to help. And every other one went off with a salmon down his trouser leg. It was the funniest sight. So there we were, stuck on the shore, with this huge pile of fish. I had to ring William Gordon-Cumming and ask him to bring a van and some boxes and come and help.

The netting was huge fun.

Sandy Edwards, the provost of Lossiemouth, was a bitter enemy of Tom Henderson's. Edwards had had the netting rights from Jimmy Dunbar of Pitgaveny - Captain James Brander Dunbar - who claimed that he was the origin of John Buchan's tale of John MacNab, the poacher. Jimmy was a great character. He argued the mouth of the River Lossie had moved eastwards, and so as he had had the netting rights from the centre of the river, westwards, he claimed rights over the whole mouth. Or maybe it was the other way round, but the result was that he claimed he owned the whole of the river's netting rights. My lease was from the crown, from the middle of the river the other way. That was from the Duke of Richmond's estate, which claimed the other half.

Consequently, whenever Sandy Edwards was fishing at the same time we were fishing, there was almost certainly going to be an argument as to whose side was being poached. These discussions frequently ended in fisticuffs. I never got involved, but Sandy and Tom used to hit each other and get really excited. It was very funny.

We also used to buy and sell lobsters and export them from Sanquhar. One day a fisherman from Loch Eriboll, right up in the North, came to the door and asked if we wanted any lobsters. I asked how many he'd got. "Ah well," he said, "I've a few." I asked him how many a few was. "Ah well, it's a few," he said. He wouldn't tell me exactly how many. So I told him he'd better bring them in. He opened the boot of his car and it was stuffed full of lobsters. That was fine. We weighed them, and I bought them. As I was unloading them, two other cars appeared at the bottom of the drive, saw that number one had got a reception, so they came along, too. So we had three cars, each full of lobsters, and by this time it was about two or three o'clock on a Thursday afternoon. They had to be packed up in wood wool, boxed and labelled and invoiced in order to get them into the Paris Les Halles for the Friday morning market. That meant catching the aeroplane at four or four thirty.

I reckoned I just had time to buy the first lot of lobsters and get them into the boxes and to the airport. But with these extra lobsters I couldn't get the whole lot done. So I eventually abandoned the idea of trying to get them to Paris for Friday. Then it transpired there was no Saturday market in Paris, and Billingsgate wasn't working either. So there was nothing for it but to cook these bloody things.

We had 750 pounds of lobster, or more, and used every receptacle in the house to boil these bloody things. There were lobsters crawling around all over the floor, and the house smelt for about a month. Dhileas who was ill at the time, had a bedroom at the top of the stairs at the back of the kitchen and she couldn't eat lobster for years afterwards. But we did cook them and sold them cooked or frozen. We managed to sell them all. I think we got out of it alright, but we didn't actually make much money for our trouble.

The prawns we were catching were another tale. I was crossing on the ferry to Skye one winter's night and the ferryman asked me if I could give someone a lift. John Morrison got in and we were chatting away, and he told me he was catching half-pound prawns. I did not believe him, so he invited me to meet his skipper in Kyle, Billy Finlayson. Finlayson had two boats - the Sweet Home, and a half share in the Castle Moil. He had made friends with a Yorkshire man called Leakey, who was a diver. Leakey had tied himself behind the boat when it was trawling, and he'd discovered the trawl was cutting through the mud. The prawns, alarmed, were slipping into the mud and leaving their claws in an upright position. The trawl was then coming along and cutting them in half. It was catching quite a lot, but killing most of them.

On learning this, Billy Finlayson decided a creel would be the way to catch prawns, so he invented the Leakey Creel. This was a lobster pot effectively, but wire framed and with a much smaller mesh. It was quite light but it would sink. He tied fifty of these things together with a bit of a gap between them and went off looking for forty fathoms of water with a muddy bottom. And he started catching live prawns. He was the first person to do it.

I went out in the boat with Leakey to watch what he was doing. On the way home he tore the tails off them all. I told him he could not do that, because the tails were wonderful on these big half pound whacking things. So I said I would take them and flog them for him. I turned out to be the first person to get live langoustine into the market at Paris. They'd never seen live ones before. And that has now become the standard method of fishing. You see prawn pots all over the place now.

I think he thought up the idea but someone else developed it. Billy Finlayson's son, Finlay, now has the restaurant in Fort William called Crannog, which is about the best seafood restaurant on the West coast.

I saw John Morrison, the chap I gave a lift to, for years after that. He lived at Luib, opposite Scalpay. I was over in Skye quite a lot at that time, buying lobsters. My brother Ewan had The Minch Shipping and Trading Company based in St James, London. But we didn't really see eye to eye. He had a chap in Portree who was buying lobsters and keeping them in a store pot in the bay after he'd bought them. Overnight they'd be stolen and sold back to him the next day. He could never understand why he was never making any money.

I had been employing Bob Bennett to drive a van up the river to collect and buy the rod-caught salmon. In doing that I became privy to extremely valuable information. I knew how many salmon were being caught on every beat on the Spey, which was secret information. I suppose we could have made more use of it for Bob had all the ghillies eating out of his hand. Cecil Moores, Mr Littlewood's Pools, owned the fishing at Elchies. His ghillie, Jimmy Milne, was a great friend of mine. He was a very good fisherman and a good ghillie, but he did like the bottle. One day I was driving the van myself. Usually, when Jimmy would give me the weights – "that is a ten pounder, that is a seven pounder", I would never question him. On this occasion Jimmy wasn't there and instead the owner of the beat, Cecil Moores was. I can't remember how it happened but Moores accused me of cheating. I was absolutely furious and he nearly went in the river. But I left, steaming. He was a very unattractive man. Perhaps that's how he made all his money.

The van probably did about a hundred-mile round trip, and it didn't cost much to run. We were probably making two or three pounds a fish and it was fun. We were dealing with very nice people on the whole and the ghillies were all absolutely splendid, but some of the guests were pretty hellish.

If you pay two or three thousand pounds a week to fish a really good stretch of river, you don't want to have to bother with carting the fish about afterwards. You want to take one home at the end of the week and put it on the slab, or maybe you want it smoked, but you don't want to have to hassle too much. You want to go back after fishing and sit down and have a dram.

It was the same with game. I never did anything with deer, because that really needed a much heavier outfit. But pheasants, grouse and woodcock particularly, were very valuable and one really could not get enough. Not only was it fun, but it involved travel abroad and in fact, that was how the family went skiing every year. We would take a box of smoked salmon and I would spend the first day flogging it. That would produce the cash for skiing. In those days, if you turned up at the back door of a good hotel and met the chef, they would usually pay cash as it would probably be cheaper, and certainly fresher, than they could get from the normal suppliers.

I do enjoy selling that way. Our dentist at that time, Adam Thompson, from Randolph Crescent in Edinburgh, was normally very expensive but never, ever charged us for his services. A duck or two, or a smoked salmon would do the trick and that was that. He had a huge income, but in the days of the Labour government's very high taxation, he also had a huge tax bill, so this sort of barter arrangement worked beautifully for us all!

***

About this time, Christopher Mackintosh, my father-in-law, was in trouble. I had to rescue him from Belgium where whatever he had been doing had gone so wrong that he was literally on his uppers. I had to put him in the boot of my Jaguar to get him out of the country where he had done all sorts of things he should not have.

Of course, having got him out, I then tried to find him something to do. He was a brilliant linguist, so he offered to be my agent in Paris and secure the sales for Salmon and Game. He told me that he would make the contacts, but I was to be responsible for checking their credentials. So he found Comptoire D'Approvisionnement de Paris - CAP. CAP traded at Les Halles and confirmed they wanted to buy my product.

I did all the checks I was supposed to do and got a two thousand pound limit from the Government Export Credit Guarantee Department (ECGD). This meant I was covered for shipping two thousand pounds worth of stuff, but not more.

By this time I was buying prawns, as I was there for the beginning of the prawn fishing industry, and was shipping all this lovely stuff - lobsters, prawns, grouse, woodcock, salmon everything, to Paris. The buyer at CAP praised the shipments, promised me a good price and over three weeks I ended up shipping him £10,000 worth of goods... which in those days was a lot of money.

Every morning I would telephone and ask for the money, and he would always reassure me it was coming. The bill ran up and up and eventually I realised that he was not going to pay and so I stopped supplying him. But by this time I was ten thousand pounds out of pocket and all these fishermen and other suppliers needed to be paid.

***

That was a very bad time. Suddenly my business, even if it was a Ltd. company, was in danger of going bankrupt. Five friends, Hector Laing, William Gordon-Cumming, Sandy Laing and Pat Wills called a meeting under the chairmanship of Iain Tennant. They said they could not allow this and would arrange a bail out. Hector Laing's lawyer then flew up from Edinburgh and produced enough cash so that I could pay my suppliers. I then issued a writ against CAP.

At about this time, the Scalberts, who were great friends of Sheena's, came to stay at Sanquhar. Raymond Scalbert, of the Banque Scalbert, a small private French bank, with another great friend, Guy Magnan took charge. Guy worked for the Banque de Paris et des Pays-Bas and recommended his lawyer, Maitre Loyrette. Loyrette listened to my tale in the Avenue Georges V and I liked him immediately. I told him that I had no money, so he said he would take the case, and if he won, he would charge 50%, but if he failed, he would charge nothing. I shook his hand and so we were off.

Six years later, after five bankruptcy actions in the French courts, we recovered the full ten thousand pounds. I had some friends in Paris who had been in the Resistance at that time and they were able to follow what was happening to the money, for each time we won a case it was moved from pillar to post. Finally we caught up with it and Loyrette charged his £5,000, to which I said that he had earned every penny, and honour was satisfied.

Everybody was paid what they were owed and that was the end of the story. But it had been a very difficult time and I had lost a good deal of confidence in the concept and in myself. Salmon & Game Services of Scotland had been a great way to do the things I enjoyed doing, and at the same time to provide a useful service. Exporting from Scotland and travelling were fun, but after this early crisis, I abandoned the business. The man who ran off with the money was very plausible, but actually the whole industry was full of crooks. Sheena had completely lost faith in the whole thing and I suppose I had too. My relationship with my father-in-law and concern about his own circumstances, were now quite a considerable problem too.

When I worked at Lloyds, the word "Fidencia" was written over the front door, meaning Good Faith. I remember that - even without the Latin crib. The whole essence at Lloyds was that if you failed to keep your word, you were out. Integrity and honesty were the watchwords, and anybody who did not measure up was finished. But then suddenly I was out in the big wide word, dealing with fish in France and it was a totally different approach to life. If the French felt they could cheat you they would do so and of course, they didn't have the slightest intention of sticking to their word.

I had been naive, and it was a very rude shock to come down to earth in that way. It had been great fun and was an enterprising business and under different circumstances I could perhaps have made more of it, but the cash crisis was certainly a big dent to my pride. I suppose I could have continued with it, but in 1966 I decided to take over the management of the caravan site as a full time occupation instead, to see what I could do with that business...

It was not long after that time that Elizabeth, Christopher's then wife (they had come to live in a flat at Sanquhar), took her two children off to the beach. Their car became stuck in the sand and we received a message saying they needed help. The house was full of guests and we were supposed to be taking them all to the Northern Meeting Ball that evening so, in a very bad temper, I took Christopher off to rescue them, with Iona, my daughter, in the back. I drove much too fast, went off the road, and turned the car upside down. Iona was thrown out and died in hospital. It was entirely my fault for which I shall never, ever forgive myself. Over the years, I have tried to obliterate the memory of that ghastly event......... but it has never worked.

After that, I'd had enough of my father-in-law and he left Sanquhar, minus an ear from the crash. Jacky Shaw Stewart took him on, even though I said don't do it. But Jacky was a much better Christian than me, or most men.

Dunconusk, Covesea and Silver Sands Holiday Park

I now retreated into the caravan business - the manager was due for the chop anyway. I had bought, during that time, a house called Dunconusk which was quite a large mansion at the edge of Lossiemouth. It had belonged to a doctor who had turned the garden and grounds into a small caravan park, with about 20 caravans.

I turfed all the caravans out and put them down at Covesea, a couple of miles away and turned the house into flats. When our own financial crisis struck us (the Paris loss), I was all for leaving Sanquhar and going to live in one of the caravans, but Sheena objected to this. I told her that I had lost a great deal of money and wanted to cut our costs and pull myself up by my bootstraps. I was down but I wanted to get up again as fast as I bloody well could, and the way to do that was to cut the illusion of great prosperity at Sanquhar and let everyone know our true state. But Sheena wouldn't agree at all, she wanted stability, particularly for the children and perhaps she was right.

Sheena with Dhileas

I wanted to impart to the children, who by this time were at boarding school, the feeling that we'd had a serious reverse and we were going to pull ourselves up, roll up our sleeves and to hell with appearances. I knew I would get back on my feet very quickly and I wanted to exaggerate the effort. But Sheena, understandably I suppose, wanted stability for the family and to keep up appearances. I do not want to criticise her, for I can see her point of view, but she was just not prepared to slum it, even though I was saying it would only have been for a few months. But all it meant in the end was that it took a bit longer to get back up than it otherwise would have done.

Honour was eventually restored, although we had to get some help from friends for school fees. Tom Lees came forward for Dhileas. I'd made him a member of Lloyds and he'd made a great deal of money from that, but I don't think that had much to do with it, because he had no obligation at all. He was a very religious person and so a very kind and generous. Uncle Geordie Selkirk paid for Alasdair, and I managed to do Duncan, albeit with some help from my mother.

It was difficult to accept, but I was pushed and had no option. In Tom's case, I was very, very grateful to him. It was an act of pure generosity. And Uncle Geordie was a childless uncle and I hope he could afford it, but nonetheless, that too was extremely generous and thoughtful of him.

At the time there was a demand from the Naval Air Station at Lossiemouth for accommodation. They hadn't room for everyone, so the residential side of the caravan business quickly became really quite profitable. And the touring side was money for old rope. The real problem on the site was drainage. We could get rid of the solid matter all right, but we couldn't get rid of the water because we were right down by the sea and the water table was very close to the surface. The water we put down into the sand would not escape and clogged up. To get the water running out to sea was going to be expensive. That was our main problem.

It was a very beautiful place. Miles of sandy beach and we had 20-30 acres among the dunes, which separated campers from the sea. We ran sand yachting and did up a cave below a lighthouse, which we ran as a nightclub. We had rows of residential caravans, nearly 100 at one time, each connected to electricity and water. Then there was a shop, a bar, and tourists came with tents and their one objective was to spend money.

I was told when I started the thing, not to have the Glasgow Fair people at the caravan park, because they were a rough sort of people. Hearing this, I thought that's exactly the sort of people I'd like to have! So when everyone else was turning them down, I encouraged them. They were tremendous and absolutely splendid. They had a horrible life for most of the year, but saved up for their holiday, and then they just spent. They were great fun and very amusing people.

About 750 Jehovah's Witnesses descended on us once and booked up every bit of accommodation we had. By day they were all witnessing away. After dark, they would come to the back door of the club and try and buy drink. But they could not be seen to be going in through the front door. They used our swimming pool for baptisms.

The cave underneath the lighthouse had become silted up with sand from the shore. I thought it would be quite fun to empty it, so I hired a bulldozer and told the driver to move as much sand as he could in a day. I bought four large huts that the navy were selling and put the floors into the cave (and then sold the huts, without floors for the same fifty pounds I had paid for them). I bought barrels, and put them in as tables, with some logs to sit on. I then built a roof with tree trunks held up against the rock face, and covered it with an orange hayrick net with an eight-inch mesh. I covered that with a black plastic sheet, then covered that with turf, so that from the outside you could not see what was going on inside.

Inside there was now a very big dance floor, which could hold up to 200 people. It was lit with candles on the cave wall and on the tables. I found Bobby Colgan's and Lindsay Ross's bands, who had become popular on the radio. The campsite itself already had a social club with a licence to sell drink until 11pm. After that time it could be "carried out". So we took the club to the cave after 11pm. It became our nightclub.

It was a memorable place and very good fun. Except for the night I got mugged by characters from Lossiemouth who thought I had the takings on me. They pulled my jersey up over my head and I landed up with a black eye. But apart from that there were no disturbances and it considerably boosted the social clubs takings.

One day the police told me I was technically selling drink after hours, because I was charging an entrance fee to the cave. So we applied for a licence. However this meant all sorts of sanitary arrangements in place of what had been happening (everyone going out and having a pee on the shore). Installing sanitary arrangements in the cave didn't make sense, so the club in the cave had to come to an end. But it had been great fun for the two to three years it lasted.

The Kennedy family, who used to come to the park from Glasgow - part of the Glasgow Fair people - were absolutely splendid. Little Donald was knee high to a grasshopper and a huge character. He worked for Rolls Royce in Hillingdon. One evening Wee Donald insisted on borrowing my kilt and came into the club with it reaching right down to his ankles...

which was terribly funny. The Glasgow Fair produced all sorts of very interesting people such as those who were building the QE2 from John Brown's yard. Later they sent me an invitation to come to the launch - down in the yard with the boys - which very sadly I was unable to do.

They led a pretty difficult life, but you couldn't defeat them. They were the salt of the earth. They were like the London cockney, absolutely indefatigable. The more difficult the circumstances, the funnier and more splendid they became.

They had saved all their money and their one object was to spend it all on holiday. I sold them all their food and they cooked in their caravans. Then we would provide some sort of entertainment. We even had an Entertainments Officer, Ali Ross, who also taught skiing at Gordonstoun.

A few years ago I was sailing with my old friend Jock McLeod with whom I had been brought up in Skye. We were anchored in Loch Torridon when a lovely little boat came up alongside and greeted Jock. Who should it be but Ali Ross? We had a very funny meeting and it turned out that he is now a ski instructor in the Alps in the winter and he sails all summer.

On the sand dunes at Covesea, next to the campsite, we organised stock car racing. We built a track and then these contraptions came along - local people had built their own machines - to race. They were amazing contraptions, all recovered scrap. They went very fast and had frightful crashes. It started when someone asked if he could try his old banger on the track, and it immediately became a great attraction. Yet again, in the end the council put paid to it on grounds of safety. I suppose it was pretty dangerous. Especially for the spectators. The posh residents of Lossiemouth thought it was a bit down market, but as far as we were concerned it was very funny.

I bought myself a sand yacht. It was designed as a DN class ice yacht. The axle was a laminated wooden axle with a bow in it, to give it some spring. That was the only bit that really mattered. Several other sand yachts emerged and we used to race them on the beach. Later I bought a sand yacht kit and Patrick Shaw Stewart said he'd build it and run it at St Andrews. Then he somehow asked for the other one as well, so he could race, and I never saw them again. And I want them back!

At one time Covesea was one of the biggest caravan parks in Scotland with up to 1,500 caravans, but the drainage problem inhibited it. It needed a maceration plant and a way of shipping it out to sea so eventually, when we absolutely had to do something about that, we decided to sell the campsite.

I sold it in 1972 for a good six-figure sum. It produced a very good return on the whole project for William Gordon-Cumming and for me.

***

Le Scots Shop

One day, when selling smoked salmon in Switzerland, I was sitting on a bench in Villars watching the ice hockey when an American man, with whiskers on his cheek, sat down beside me and started talking American. I said I'd come from Scotland, and he said - Do you know Charles Ray-nald? I said I'd never heard of Charles Ray-nald. Then it occurred to me that "Ray-nald" spoken with an American drawl could possibly be "Ranald" spoken without one. There was a fellow called Ranald who was a relation of ours. He was actually born Ezekiel, but he changed his name to Ranald, quite wisely I think. And his descendent was called Charles, who was christened Charles Gesto after the house in Skye we all come from.

It turned out Charles was in Villars, and we decided to go and meet him. So we went along to this fellow's house, and discovered that indeed he was a relation. Charles Gesto had been sacked from Harrow and had gone to Smithfield, from where he had been sacked again, and then had gone somewhere else, where he'd also been sacked. He went to the City and became a clerk, invented unit trusts, formed the Britannia Unit Trust, which he then sold for a million pounds. He had bought a house in Villars, which he got David Hicks to decorate, with carpets which were two or three inches thick. He was an entertaining character with a "bidie in" too: Caroline, a rather attractive girl.

We had some laughs together over a lunch or a dinner and during the conversation I said I thought it would be quite fun to have a shop abroad to sell Scottish things. He said he had also thought of doing that, and that he had a house in Port Grimaud, where he suggested we open a shop. Which we did. We opened "Le Scots Shop" in Port Grimaud to sell Scottish products, and actually ended up selling thick jerseys and kilts to people who were mostly topless and it did not really work. There was a factory in Inverness making cashmere jerseys, which went bust because the cashmere was faulty. I bought all the stock of cashmere jumpers which just did not fit properly, and sold them for a huge profit in our shop.

On one occasion I was being a bit too clever. I brought the stock down to the South of France by plane, but decided not to bother to declare it to customs. I was caught, had awful trouble and was put on the blacklist and charged with smuggling for which I had to pay quite a fine.

Le Scots Shop, which was opposite Brigitte Bardot's house, was fun. The clothes did not fit the customers properly and it made no money. I think it would have worked if we had done it in the Alps, but he had this place and we thought it would be amusing. It was really just an excuse to go to Port Grimaud. So that was another slightly pointless exercise, which Duncan dates at 1976, (the year he was rusticated from Fettes).

***

In the summers we would visit Skye, or the Shaw Stewarts at Linplum in East Lothian, in the winters we would go skiing. We did not have adventures like Alasdair is having now with his family. He has recently taken them white water rafting and walking in the Himalayas.

We would amuse ourselves. Sheena instigated a lot of plays at Sanquhar and used to have an annual reel party in the ballroom, which would commence with several local families joining in to put on a short play or a few skits in the next-door dining room, which had a sort of stage area. I don't really like acting, but Sheena loves it, and is good at it. I wasn't but would usually be dragged in, so on the odd occasion thought I might do something a bit different. One time they had decided to put on The Sugar Plum Fairy. There were artificial marble pillars across one bit of the room and a moulding at the top where I reckoned I could rig a pole. From this I thought I could suspend a rope. The pillars became the front of the stage where the curtains were going to be drawn in and out in front of the stage area.

I rigged the pole, and managed to get quite a large, thick rope fixed to the centre and pulled up to one side and anchored to a stepladder. I'd estimated that when the rope swung down, tied around my tummy, it would swing more or less clear of the floor. I climbed up the ladder and suspended myself from this rope, dressed up as a fairy, holding a wand, in the most obscene outfit. I had a blond wig, a wand, little dancing pumps on my feet, a low cut tutu with my rather hairy legs jutting out below.

The Sugar Plump Fairy with Sallly Mackintosh and Dhileas

At the given moment I set forth from the top of the stepladder and swung into the middle of the stage in front of the audience of about 100 local friends with their families. I swung backwards and forwards holding this wand before I realised I couldn't stop. And when I finally stopped swinging to and fro, I realised I couldn't reach the ground. So I was dangling from this bloody thing, holding the wand, and oh dear, it was a terrible moment. A thick rope around my tummy and my hands and feet dangling down at about the same level.

There was a frightful creaking sound as the pole groaned under my weight. Even worse, the rope started to twizzle round, so the audience ended up looking straight up between my legs. And all this time I was shouting - "shut the bloody curtains".

Of course, the family was laughing so much, they couldn't shut them. Eventually they had to cut me down. The Sugar Plum Fairy. It completely ruined the play. Everyone fell off their chairs laughing though.

One very cold winter at Sanquhar, we woke one morning to find the loch in front of us was frozen. There was an island in the middle of the loch and a pony had walked across the ice and got onto the island. We were worried that if the ice melted and the pony was left on the island, there wouldn't be any food for it. So the puzzle was how to get it back.

We considered the matter and decided to summon the fire brigade. They came instantly. They rushed up with the bells clanging amid great excitement. Their leader came up to assess the problem, and when I told him there was a pony stuck on the island, he immediately sprang into action. His team, about three of them, set off across the ice to retrieve the pony, and promptly fell through the ice.

So the firemen left on the shore had to rescue them. They put a ladder across the ice and set out on it. Then the ladder went through the ice.

By the end of it, pretty nearly the whole fire brigade was in the water. But they made such a mess of the ice, there was a hole which the pony could swim back through. This was all at eight o'clock in the morning, and after it all they all had to come into the house for a dram. We gave them a very good whisky.

Roger Wellesley-Smith came to stay another time there was a lot of snow on the ground for Christmas or New Year. There was snow everywhere, and we went out to dinner. When we came back, I went off to put the car in the garage and Sheena and Roger went into the house. The door had a Yale lock, and when I got back, the whole place was locked up. I couldn't get in.

I decided to go round to the room Roger was sleeping in and chuck a snowball up to attract his attention. This I did and he flung the window up. 'Oh', he said. 'You're locked out, are you?' And he jumped out himself and then we were both locked out. But perhaps that sort of loyalty was questionable?

Another memory from when we lived at Sanquhar related to my brother, Ewan. He had an office in St.James's, just off Jermyn Street, London. I went to see him one late afternoon and put my car on a meter in St James's Square. I put enough money to take the meter up to six o'clock. They ran out at half past six, but I thought I'd take a chance on the last half hour. When I came out at just after seven or something, no car. I rang the police and told them my car had been stolen. They replied that they were very sorry, but it had been towed away to the Elephant and Castle car pound. I thought, the hell with that, so in a filthy temper I got in a taxi and went to the car pound.

When I got there, I flung the door of the office open, to make a sort of entry, and told them that I thought the police were splendid, but that they shouldn't steal my car. A voice from the North East of Scotland asked what the number was, which I gave him. He said that it sounded like a Morayshire number and I replied that it was. I gave him my name, and he asked if I lived at Sanquhar. I said that I did. Oh, he said. I used to work in the estate office. So we had a splendid conversation about local affairs and eventually I told him I was going. He said that I would have to pay the fine. I told him not to be silly. After talking like that, I was not going to pay a fine. And anyway, he shouldn't have stolen my car. He said that if I refused to pay the fine, I must write to the head man, and here was his address.

So I wrote to the head policeman telling him I respected the police and appreciated they had a difficult time, but I really didn't think they should go around stealing cars. I added it was quite unnecessary to take it for half an hour over the time limit, that I hated coming to London anyway, and having had my car stolen had made it worse than usual. The only redeeming feature was the nice man I'd met in the office. I finished the letter saying I was very sorry, but would not be paying the fine.

I got a letter back saying - so glad to hear you don't come to London very often, they didn't like towing away cars and so on. I could see he had quite a sense of humour, because he finished his letter, saying that he was very sorry, but I must pay the fine. I wrote back, making a lot more facetious remarks, finishing, once again, - So I'm very sorry, but I will not be paying the fine. And it went on like this for several weeks. We got quite a correspondence going. Finally, he wrote saying that he'd spent so much money on stamps, he'd better call this off. So I never did pay!

***

Talking of cars, my loony, but-splendid old aunt Catriona, known as Tushki had a tale or two. She was my mother's sister and was quite a character. When we were living at Sanquhar she often came to see us. She was a considerable eccentric. She owned two Rolls Royce's and had a long-suffering chauffeur, Frank, but no money to speak of. She used to arrive driving one Rolls and Frank driving the other, with both cars loaded with all sorts of extraordinary junk.

Later a good salesman persuaded her to trade in her Rolls for a brand new Amphicar. After that she would travel around Scotland in this thing, sitting imperiously in the back with Frank at the wheel. Whenever they got back to Skye, they would drive straight past the ferry queue into the sea and chug across to the other side. On one occasion an American tourist fainted at the sight of this. But Tushki did rather like style and she had plenty of it. Unfortunately, she had failed to read the small print about how to use the Amphicar though, which actually specified it was not meant to go in the sea. So much to her disappointment, the thing rotted away to nothing in an incredibly short time.

One day at Sanquhar, she asked if she could have a packet of cornflakes, which had an Ideal Home competition publicised on the back. She then cut it up to make it into the model of the sort of house she wanted to build. She applied for planning permission, and the planning people said they were sorry, but they needed a drawing, not a model. So we went off and got a drawing done.

She had selected a spot down at the south end of Skye by Tocavaig, which must be one of the most beautiful sites in Skye, between the road and the sea, absolutely lovely. She got planning permission, and eventually started building. Half way through she decided to have another window here, and another window there and a tower and so on. When it was finished it bore absolutely no resemblance to the plan. There were fourteen extra windows, and a tower.

My father was chairman of the planning committee at this time, so he had the embarrassing job of trying to tell my aunt that she had to remove the tower, although she couldn't do much about the windows.

The house was eventually finished. It was built mostly of wood and was actually rather nice and fun. It was in a magical spot. When she died it was left to my cousin Catriona Wroughton and to me. Catriona took it over and spent a lot more money on it. It is lovely now.

I used to go and see Tushki, to make sure she was all right, because she lived by herself. I was staying with her one spring when I decided to visit Eilean Ruaraidh, an island not far away, with a ruined castle, to look for gulls eggs. I had my dog with me and we rowed out in the dinghy. We couldn't find any eggs and I was just sitting about on the island examining my navel, not really thinking about anything much, when an otter came towards me with something in its mouth - a sort of white object. I sat absolutely still and he swam up to just below me, about ten yards away, climbed onto a rock and started eating an octopus. Chewing all the tentacles off, one by one. I sat and watched, absolutely riveted and thought I'd see if I could get a bit closer. I got back in the dingy from behind the hill and I let the wind take me round so I could bump up against the rock and have a close look at the otter. Eventually he looked up and realised I was there and slipped back into the sea, leaving the octopus behind, which I'm afraid to say I pinched and took home and had for tea. It was lovely watching the otter. I've seen others. It is possible to see them at least once a year swimming in the sea.

As for gull's eggs, that's probably illegal now. But we used to collect small black headed gulls eggs perfectly legally, and plovers eggs. When plovers eggs were outlawed, black headed gulls eggs became the thing, as black headed gulls were a bit of a nuisance.

***

In about 1961, as we were moving north to Sanquhar, I became involved with naval noughts and crosses. This was a game invented by Admiral Denis Campbell, the Admiral who saved the aircraft carrier from being scrapped by designing the angled flight deck. He was a very interesting man. I met him through Mike Fell, a Captain who was commanding the Naval air station at Lossiemouth. They had a game, which I think the Navy had played, of four-dimensional noughts and crosses which was four squares wide on four separate planes. You could draw a line vertically through four lines, or you could do four diagonal lines through the whole of the four floors. Or you could do any one of the horizontal lines on the four separate planes. It was quite a testing game.

Denis Campbell claimed he had the world manufacturing rights. Which he gave to me for one year. During that year I tried to make the game and then sell it. Harrods wanted a hundred percent mark-up and I couldn't make it for less than five pounds. Harrods wanted to sell it for less than ten pounds, so on that basis, I had to abandon it. But for a time, it looked like a rather splendid fortune around the corner.

At one stage at Sanquhar, William Gordon-Cumming tried to let his grouse moor and I said I would try to organise a shoot. We had Russ Aitken, an American, whose wife was a princess. He'd shot things all over the world so was very full of himself, but he'd never shot grouse. I can remember giving everyone a lecture on the lawn at Sanquhar before the first shoot. I said they had to be very careful, that they must shoot to the front and that it was very easy to swing through the line, but if anyone did swing through the line, they would be sent home at once.

On the first drive Russ Aitken followed a hare through the line. I couldn't really send him home, so instead gave him a really good bollocking which he didn't like at all from a whippersnapper like me. But when he did it a second time, I did send him home. He was furious and got very cross indeed. But he was very definitely dangerous, so it was the right thing to do. There are a lot of these sort of people who are very rich and think they can do what they like. But he was one who did actually come back. He was a very nice chap, actually. However I did not enjoy running a commercial shoot, so soon gave it up. There is a completely different atmosphere to going out with your friends. Out with friends you have no inhibitions. But somehow or other, if you pay a lot of money, it alters the sense of the whole thing.

Our time at Sanquhar eventually had to come to an end. William Gordon-Cumming had always said he was going to knock the house down and develop the area. It had been made perfectly clear to me from the start, so even after ten or twelve years, I could accept it. But Sheena could not. She made a terrible song and dance about it. Quite wrongly, I think.

CHAPTER EIGHT

Logie Farm and Highland Wine

So we left Sanquhar House in the spring of 1973 and while we were looking for the next HQ, we rented Tarras Farm House, just outside Forres, from Hamish White. It had no land attached so there was no farming necessary. Sheena was always keen to have something to do with horses – even though they had pretty well ruined all the trees in the Sanquhar House garden, so we went looking for a house with land.

I think you could say that I am prepared to try and do almost anything, including hunting or riding, but I hate riding horses seriously. The last time I went hunting was with the Surrey Union, or the Surrey Onions as they were known, when we lived at Little Benhams. We had been out all day and had not caught a fox, so I thought it was time to go home. We started to return but inadvertently walked in front of the hounds, an apparently unforgivable error at which point the Master swore at Sheena. So I turned round and told him not to bloody well speak to my wife like that.

There was an awful hush and no one quite knew which way to look, so we trotted off down the road. Sometime later the Master came charging down the road after us, and, grinding to a halt in front of me, said - "Young man, I don't think you know who I am." I just said: "I know perfectly well who you are, and I do not expect you to speak to my wife like that." But I didn't have quite the right answer for him and all the way back home, I kept thinking of better replies that I might have made.

Two or three days later it happened that I was driving through Rusper on a tractor with a fork lift on the front. The hunt appeared, led by the same Master, and I couldn't resist it so I lowered the forklift, and raised it up to him like a giant V-sign. To give him his due, he raised his hat to me, so we had a good laugh; but I am afraid I feel they did always take themselves rather too seriously.

***

We found Logie Farm in early 1974. It had about 100 acres in the Findhorn valley, just downstream from Glenferness, in Nairnshire. It is a very beautiful hill farm, with a long rough drive of nearly a mile taking you in. It is bordered by forestry on one side and the River Findhorn running for about a mile on the other. It had once been part of the Leven estate. The farmer who sold it, Mr Manson, had worked it for most of his life, but I don't think he realised quite what a gem he had. Once he had seen it, my old friend Hugh Cawdor was especially keen that we got it and he went to enormous trouble to see that we did. He even went as far as buying two fields to help us with the purchase. I believe he also went around any of the local landowners who were showing an interest and leaned on them pretty heavily not to compete for it. I shall always be grateful to him for being so helpful to us at that time – a true friend.

The farm had a small farmhouse (including a tiny fourth bedroom they described as "The Former Maid's Room") that stood high above the river, but was not big enough for our needs. Next to the farmhouse there were some attractive and substantial stone-built steading buildings. There was also a dilapidated cottage that sat lower down, but on a bluff above a bend in the river at the far end of the farm. I initially wanted to do that up as our main house - it would have been a magic spot, but my old friend Jamie Dunbar Nasmith, who had become quite a prominent architect, said that converting the steading would be a much cheaper option; so we went for that instead. He appointed a partner, Jack Buchanan to do it for us.

When testing the strength of some of the floorboards, Jack went straight through, landing with one leg on each side of a beam with nails in it. I am not too sure what that would have done to his prospects... but rather him than me!

There was a considerable water problem - we had to bring in a new supply involving pumping the water up from a well about a hundred feet below the house. That was the first of our problems. There had been a ram pump on the hill, the principle of which is that very high pressure at one point drives the water up, and of course Jack had to test it. Inevitably he got himself absolutely soaked. He was not very efficient but he was a very nice man and he and Jamie did do a fine job designing the house from the old steading, and the cottage as well.

Eventually, under Jack's guidance, we finished the Steading House conversion and, for once in our lives, we had a modern, well-built, comfortable and functional home. My plan was to farm it, (keeping some ground for Sheena's horses), while keeping an eye out for other opportunities to spread my wings from there.

Once, soon after we got the place, I saw a roe buck feeding on the roadside as we approached the house. When it heard us, it took off and tried to get through the wire fence, but it got stuck. I was able to jump out, kill it with a knife and take it home to eat. That seemed a good start.

However, farming at Logie quickly became difficult. The grass didn't start until a month later than lower down, it also finished earlier. Similar conditions applied to crops. It was clearly not going to be much use as a farm. It only took me two or three years to realise that I was not going to make it as a farmer - and consequently I now had too much capital tied up in it, because there wasn't enough cash available to apply to anything else. I soon decided we had bitten off more than we could chew and found myself somewhat stranded.

During this time, looking to generate income, I became involved with Moniack Wineries. This was Philippa Fraser's home grown Highland wine from Moniack Castle, near Inverness. I took on sales for the Highlands alongside Scrap Balfour-Paul, a brother officer of Sandy Fraser in Lovat Scouts during the war.

Years before I had tried to persuade Sandy and Philippa to come and live at Moniack, long before they actually did. The castle needed much restoration for it had been badly run down, but Sandy was good fun and adventurous, with a splendid view on life. He forecast that Highland Wineries would have a limited future and would attract competition, so he thought he had four years before he would sell the business and then do something else.

Before moving back to Moniack, Philippa and Sandy had been farming in Suffolk. The farm had a huge grain mixing machine into which Sandy fell while it was still operating. It was finally stopped; but by that time he was quite badly hurt, and crippled. Then he got Parkinson's disease.

I should actually have had shares in the Moniack Winery, but when I discussed it with Jacky Shaw Stewart, he said not to touch it with a barge pole. As it turned out, I think he was quite wrong, for I was paid a salary based on £5 a case, and I sold over a thousand in Skye alone. It really was a jolly good business.

Sandy and Philippa were a good partnership for he had the strategy in his head and Philippa had the tactics. It was her idea that things growing wild in the Highlands could be turned into wine and she developed all the means to produce some really quite drinkable wines. She didn't particularly enjoy cooking, but she can certainly follow recipes and she should take much credit for all the many excellent sauces she has produced.

Scrap Balfour-Paul was a very old friend, who had grown apples with Sandy before he farmed in Suffolk. When Philippa asked me to help Scrap sell the wines, I entered into the spirit of the thing wholeheartedly. Both Scrap and I enjoyed working for Philippa, especially the money she paid us and the freedom to move about Scotland as we pleased. Selling a good Highland product, albeit an unusual one, made it all very good fun.

Scrap was responsible for the Highland area, which we divided up more or less according to where the fishing was. We used to set off on our selling trips, suitably armed, with a rod, and then have a bit of a Ceilidh with whoever was in our sights.

I went on a sales trip to the Outer Isles at the end of 1980 with David Shaw Stewart and was reminded of Squeaky Robertson, the skipper of the Loch Mhor, which used to run from Portree to Stornoway. He had a very high-pitched voice and on one occasion he had an Admiral on board who went up to visit Squeaky on the bridge. The Admiral was looking at the chart and asked Squeaky where he thought they were. Squeaky pointed it out, to which the Admiral said – "These marks on the chart must be dangerous waters here". "Well," said Squeaky. "If it's rocks we're buggered. But if it's fly shit, which I think it is, we'll be alright."

We called at several places south from Lochmaddy and at Ludaig at the southern end of South Uist, and we had to cross The Sound of Barra on a boat called the Very Likely, skippered by Donald Campbell. When we arrived, Donald was reading the paper. We asked if this was the ferry to Barra, and he took no notice at all. He just said "yes", without looking up. So we got on board and eventually he stopped reading the paper and joined us on board. We set off with my briefcase full of samples and so I thought I would talk to Donald to see what he thought the selling possibilities in Barra might be.

I asked "Do you think anyone in Barra would be interested in Highland Wine?" "No," said Donald. "Not at all. They only drink the hard stuff in Barra." But I noticed that over the entrance to the wheelhouse, there was a sign saying – "Marriages conducted by the captain of this ship last for the duration of the voyage only". So clearly he had a bit of a twinkle.

"Well well, that is very disappointing," I said. "I have some samples of Highland Wine here so you would not want to try them, I am sure."

"Ah well, that is quite different." he said. This caused his mother-in-law, who was also travelling on the boat, to take a bit of interest. When we reached Barra, about half an hour later, there were no samples left at all. They had drunk pretty well the whole lot.

'Pickled Herring!' by Alasdair

We sold quite a few bottles on Barra. It was great fun marching in somewhere that has never heard of you and try to sell them some Highland Wine. I used to say: "Don't drink this foreign rubbish that's made abroad, you want to drink some good Highland products". I love going somewhere new, particularly the Outer Isles, which are very beautiful and so have many amusing characters.

I never enjoyed selling insurance at Lloyds, because having married the niece of The Duke of Hamilton, my employer thought I was somebody or other of great connection and so I was used – and that made me cringe. But to sell smoked salmon in Switzerland in order to go skiing was quite a different feeling. To sell Scottish wine in Scotland is absurd -

I mean who makes wine in Scotland? To sell it in the Outer Isles is even more absurd but fun and profitable too. That was the nice thing about the whole Moniack project.

Philippa was extremely enterprising and very able. She has brought up her six children in a strong Catholic atmosphere to which she converted when she married Sandy. She has held Moniack together with the winery business and now in her dotage, expects her many offspring to look after her, which by and large, they do.

During this time of the Moniack Wines, to help with the living costs, Sheena tried make a go of an expanded riding school. It was very constructive of her, but it was not going to be of any interest to me. We struggled on for a bit, but with neither the riding school nor the wine providing enough income, for me the writing was on the wall. Sheena was convinced that I wanted to marry Philippa. My frequently repeated assurances to the contrary absolutely failed to convince her, so, encouraged by several sympathisers for her cause, she divorced me.

I had attempted to reassure her as best I could that money was really our problem and that we could no longer afford to keep Logie Farm and we needed to sell it, but she was adamant that it was too important to sell and so, very stupidly, in 1982 we parted. She stayed at Logie and I went to Skye.

CHAPTER NINE

Move Back To Skye

I bought Burnside Cottage at Glen Bernisdale when I moved to Skye in 1982. It was part of the old Keeper's Cottage that Jock Urquhart lived in when I was a boy. It was fairly dilapidated and very small, but Alec Shaw Stewart helped me greatly with its restoration. It became my new base for operations. I had a little bit of money available and so I also bought some property at Greshornish from Donald Matheson. Developing all that became my chief activity for my new start back in Skye, as well as with fighting a battle with The Forestry Commission over trees on the Edinbane estate.

The Edinbane estate, which my father left to me in his will when he died in 1974 (and Tayinloan jointly to me and my brother Ewan), is a little under 2,000 acres on the North West side of Skye, near Dunvegan, with 29 crofting tenants on it. The tenants are largely old friends of mine and of the family. My father was born in Edinbane and it had been in the family for a long time (although my father himself had actually bought it from his cousin, Roddy Robertson-MacLeod).

Shortly after I inherited, Dan MacNab, the Township Clerk came to me and asked why I was putting up a fence on the hill. I knew nothing about it, so we all walked up to look and discovered that The Forestry Commission, who were planting trees on Department of Agriculture land at Glenvicaskill next door, had crossed our march with their fence. They had enclosed 320 acres of our Edinbane Common Grazings. Clearly they had misread the map. Alastair Henry was the Department Factor at the time and he should really have known better.

I asked my solicitor, Neil MacMillan, to write and tell them to remove the fence. Nothing happened for 18 months, whereupon they proceeded to plough the enclosed land and started planting trees, completely disregarding my letter.

What followed became a classic cause celebre. I had a strong case - and clear evidence - that they had ploughed our land. So, backed up by the absolutely ferret-like qualities of the Edinburgh surveyor from D M Hall, who took an immense amount of trouble to provide the necessary evidence, I got Spencer Patrick of MacLay, Murray and Spens to issue a writ against the Secretary of State and The Lord Advocate representing the Forestry Commission. It took six years for them to capitulate, which they did on the steps of the High Court. In 1984 they paid me £75,000 for the damage done. This really was a substantial sum for a crofting estate of this size.

I planned to split the money 50/50 between the Crofters and myself and asked Jeff MacLeod of MacLeod & McCallum, based in Inverness, a previous Chairman of the Crofters Commission, to act for me. To my amazement (and great disappointment) he declined to act for both sides. At Jeff's instigation, a man called Burns from Dingwall was bought into the picture. He was absolutely delighted to represent the crofters against a wicked landlord and thought he had a nice little argument on his hands, which he certainly managed to stir up. The net result was that the case had to go to the Land Court which allocated rather more than half of the money to me and less than half to the crofters, who also had to pay all the expenses. So the crofters came off much less well than they would have done if they had done what I had proposed to them in the first place. I don't think there was too much bad feeling about it, but they were pretty fed up, and I made it known that I was equally fed up myself.

***

Johnny Macdonald of Tote had been the only member of our family to believe in Skye after the war. He started milk production at Skeabost and then bought the Home Farm in Portree, where the milk production was based, and supplied the whole island with milk. But eventually he found it very hard to find enough people to get up at 4am to milk the cows and keep the business going and so it petered out. Johnny later sold the Home Farm to be developed as a housing estate. He himself went to London and set up Electro Devices, a company making electronic instruments and defence equipment. But he came back and bought the Skeabost Estate back from Duncan MacLeod. He was like an elder brother to me.

My father, although full of good ideas, really did not know how to make his ideas work. He always strongly discouraged me from trying to make it in Skye. He considered that one should make money elsewhere and then come back with the proceeds - as he had been brought up to experience.

A year or so after I arrived in Skye, Johnny offered to lease the Home Farm House to me so that I could sell Burnside Cottage for a tidy profit. Home Farm involved paying a rent, but the move made a little bit more capital available for other things, which was very helpful. Home Farm itself eventually became the great housing development that exists today, but it was very kind of Johnny to lease the farmhouse to me, and it gave me a good start.

It was at the Home Farm House that I had some trouble with Janet Macdonald. She was the wife of a nice old crofter neighbour of Aunt Catriona (known as Tushki). Janet had parted company from her rather alcoholic man, Martin, and had moved to Portree. Because she knew of my connection with Tushki, she used to walk into the house without knocking, which generally became rather a bore. One day I spotted her coming towards the house. Immediately opposite the back door, through which she was about to enter, was the loo at the end of the passage so I quickly took my trousers down and sat on the loo with the door open and waited for her to arrive. I think that stopped her coming in from then on.

I stayed in the Home Farm House for several years, until the old stables at Greshornish, which Donald Matheson had turned into a steading, came up for sale. I bought it, along with three cottages and several acres, including the foreshore for £20,000.

When our ancestor Kenneth MacLeod, who had made a lot of money in India came back to Skye in the 1800's, he built his mansion house at Greshornish out of two smaller houses. He also turned the original Tackman's house into his stables. The result was a fine old building with a good amount of space. Upstairs was a hayloft, but the floors were all rotten.

I set about doing this as my next development, intending to create a properly comfortable house to live in, with enough room to have the family to stay, along with friends as well. David Roberts was a very talented artist who had written books about architectural history. He had bought Orbost and was interested in restoring old buildings. He

Kenneth MacLeod of Greshornish, Coinneach Mhor

was responsible for my interest in what was to become The Orde of Greshornish. He did all the designs for the house and, being very much a purist, resigned three or four times during the course of our operations.

When I suggested using UPVC windows in the renovation, he said he would never speak to me again and insisted on wooden windows, painted with five undercoats of lead based paint. With hindsight, I think he was absolutely right. The original buildings were lovely and with David's inspired guidance it is now listed.

The original big house is now a hotel. While I was living at The Orde it was owned by the very unpleasant Jane Dickson with Campbell, her young son. They tried to make my life as impossible as they could. They did not like having a neighbour so close to their house.

The big house was subsequently bought by Neil and Rosie Colquhoun who are terrific, but they are currently trying to sell. Neil was a Housemaster at Eton and had run a school for expelled pupils, before attempting to become an hotelier.

The project at The Orde took me rather more than a year to complete. Matheson had owned Greshornish for quite a few years but had taken everything he could get out of the place, but put absolutely nothing back. He had not maintained the fences, or the buildings. He was really just out for what he could get.

David Roberts knew a fellow - Michael Wheatley - who lived at Waternish and was very good with all kinds of building from joinery to masonry. The Orde became a great project to work on with him. I think we made a fantastic job of it and it became a very comfortable house. The Greshornish property was a good investment, particularly as later on I was able to acquire a Right of Pre-emption over the big house, through a land deal, to add to the whole place. It gave me the right to match the best offer, if it comes on the market.

I renovated the cottages on the shore as an office for a Salmon Farm and another cottage opposite the entrance to the main house. Having won my case against the Forestry Commission, I then attacked The Crown Estate for giving salmon farm leases to big companies, arguing that locals round the shore should have preference. I eventually won my case against the Crown Estate, and got my own Salmon Farm lease at Greshornish.

Salmon farm at Greshornish

The underlying principle is that my life in Skye has been to do things with the tenants. They are a vital part of any plans I have had on the island.

As a matter of principle, I was anxious to try and convert common grazings on the hill at Edinbane, that we had lost to the Forestry Commission, to common grazings in the sea, for the crofters living around the loch. I invited all the shareholder crofters from Edinbane, who had recently been paid out from the tree battle, to participate in the fish farm. Most of them did, putting in about a quarter of the capital we had to find.

Having achieved that I needed a partner who knew about fish farming to run it. John Minaur the managing director of Highland Fish Farmers could have been a possible partner, but was not interested because I had so many shareholders. His company wanted the lease on their own. During negotiations he was extremely evasive and would not come clean about his plans.

Fed up, I approached Ian Anderson, of Jethro Tull, the pop group, fame. He had just bought the Strathaird estate, on the south end of Skye, and already had several fish farms. I invited him to come and join the battle for the lease which he did, and we made a very good arrangement. We had a right of up to 49% of the smolts in the fish farm, while Ian Anderson's team ran the whole thing with the lease jointly in Strathaird's and Edinbane Seafarms Ltd's name.

We got a Highland Board grant of £40,000 and a loan of £40,000, repayable over five years. So we had £100,000 of cash with which to buy fish and bought 30,000 smolts in the first year. Subsequently we had to have rather less than 30,000 because having repaid the loan, out of rather limited profits, but profits nevertheless, the cash available with which to buy fish, was getting low.

Running a fish farm can be high risk towards the end of a cycle because there is a time when the valuable stocks are vulnerable to disease. I felt the risk was unjustifiable for the shareholders. At the time Norway was attacking the industry by dumping fish on Europe. As it has turned out Norway has since taken over the Scottish salmon farming industry, prices have boomed and we might have done well to remain in it, with hindsight.

We had two profitable cycles, each lasting approximately 18 months. We had four cycles in all before we finally decided to pack up. The last two were not profitable and we ended up selling the company to Straithaird Estate for £50,000, with £30,000 payable in year one and two further tranches of £10,000 each, subject to the price of salmon rising. Had that price risen over the course of a year then we would have been entitled to a larger payout when Strathaird bought us out. Strathaird then sold immediately on to Marine Harvest. I was upset they did not tell me they had done this deal and intended to sell up at the time they bought from us. Marine Harvest is now Norwegian owned, as is most of the Scottish Salmon Farming industry, and it still runs the Greshornish Fish Farm.

There are those who say that the fish farm pollutes the loch, but I would argue that the tidal exchange in the loch is very strong so the droppings are very quickly dissipated. Nature has an amazing power to recover and the benefits for young people in employment from husbandry in the sea are worthwhile.

***

I lived at The Orde for this period of about three years, and it was a very comfortable place to live. It was just a bit too far from Portree to be convenient however.

I would have loved to continue there, but with the bad relationship with Jane Dickson and her son living next door and an overdraft I had built up to complete the restoration, I decided to sell.

Johnny Macdonald's sister Wytchy, who was married to Donald Cameron of Lochiel's younger brother, Colonel Charlie, had Skirinish House, right beside Tote, for many years, letting it for holidays. It has six or seven bedrooms and a cottage attached. It is in a fine site and is only six or seven minutes' drive to Portree. Wytchy and Charlie decided to give it up and move to Nairn, as they liked playing bridge and there were not many bridge partners in Skye. Charlie had been working on seaweed for Alginate Industries in the Uists, as well as standing for Parliament as a Conservative candidate, but they were both feeling rather older. Wytchy was very sad to leave Skye and it was sad they went.

Johnny then offered to let me have Skirinish on an attractive rental basis. It did need quite a lot of work on it, which I agreed to do and I enjoyed improving the house. I believe I have improved the place and have been very happy here and it has I hope been a good thing generally for the Macdonalds to have me there.

The latest Bentley

Johnny allowed me to rent the cottage just beside the house as well. I did it up and rented it out as holiday accommodation quite successfully. One year I did up the coal hole at Skirinish, like accommodation on a boat, and lived in that while I tried to let the house itself for holidays, but it was not really smart enough so I stopped, and moved into the cottage to "down size". However, it became obvious that letting the cottage for holidays was a much better bet, so I moved back into the main house again.

Last year, Marianne de Raad, a Dutch lady, took the cottage for the winter and then asked to extend her lease through the summer, so we now have her on a direct lease with Charles Macdonald, Johnny's son, and I am back in the house with no more responsibility for the cottage than making sure that she is a satisfactory tenant for Charles, and that suits me fine.

Charles Macdonald, who took over the Tote estate after Johnny died, has continued to be astonishingly supportive and both he and Juliet and all their children have been wonderful family friends. As the years have gone by, both Charles and Juliet have been astonishingly patient with me and I shall always be grateful to them and to their entire family.

I regret that my father, of whom I was very fond, did not approve of my Skye inclinations. As I have observed already, he was brought up to believe that money should be made elsewhere, and that with my background of Eton, Scots Guards, Lloyds, SAS and Sheena, it would all be wasted if I came back too soon. He lived his own life as a true servant of the Skye that he loved, so it was very sad that we did not see eye to eye over that.

He himself was in Skye during a time that there was de-population and there wasn't much hope for young people. He tried to reverse that but at the same time he tried to encourage me not to move here. But today it is a different picture with a terrific future for the island and I am so pleased that I decided not to take his advice on this.

***

Edinbane Wind Farm

The first inkling I had of anything going on was when David Still, of Border Wind, turned up asking for the exclusive rights to put an anemometer up on the hill, to measure the effects of the wind.

I enquired into what he was up to and could see there was going to be a possibility of something. Edinbane was in the area designated by the council as a possible place for a wind farm. So I told him he couldn't have exclusivity. We investigated a little more, and it emerged there were several companies who were interested in wind farming. Each had to build a picture of wind speeds and their variations over a period. As the government is keen to have more renewable energy to replace fossil fuels, it emerged that the financial possibilities were good.

One turbine, which would potentially cost up to three quarters of a million pounds to install, would yield a good rent to the owner of the land, or one or two per cent of the sale of the electricity to the grid. I investigated the possibilities with a few others who were interested and discovered we were possibly onto a winner.

David Still was starting an experimental operation through Jonny Noble of Ardkinglas in Argyllshire, who thoroughly recommended him. There was also somebody else in the Borders whom my son-in-law, Harry Lukas, knew. Border Wind at their expense then put up an anemometer on the top of our hill to measure the wind speeds for more than a year. I used my old Argo - an eight-wheeled all purpose vehicle - to put it all in place.

We put in a competitive bid to the government but failed by point something of a penny. The land thought suitable on Edinbane would probably take up to 16 turbines, but the most economical unit would be something like double that number. I considered approaching John MacLeod of MacLeod at Dunvegan and the Department of Agriculture, who also had neighbouring land, as well as a speculator who was planting trees on Coishletter, but in the meantime, the winter wind knocked the anemometer over.

The anemometer had two crossbars each of which has a wind direction indicator and a wind speed indicator. The wind speed indicator has three cups on a spindle, which revolve according to the speed of the wind. One of these cups mysteriously came off and it was thought that an eagle must have landed on it. Unfortunately the RSPB were objecting to wind farms because they believed eagles would get minced up by the revolving blades of turbines. It has always puzzled me why they think an eagle might not see a wind farm, when eagles can spot mice from hundreds of feet in the air. The anemometer was replaced and we continued to collect data. David Nelson read the meter on a regular basis for AMEC, who had taken over Border Wind.

It took 25 years, and many, many stories which I don't have room for in this tale, but we finally got planning permission for the wind farm and set up Edinbane Wind Farm Company Ltd, with eighteen 2.3Mw Enercon turbines of which we have eleven on the Edinbane Estate, and my neighbour Allan Clark has seven on GlenVicaskill. It puts out enough power for about 35,000 houses. We did it on a revenue share basis with the developer, Amec. We made half the shares available to the community of our Edinbane Crofting tenants and the other half to me or my family. The developers agreed to £50,000 a year to the local community company, so now this remote community has achieved something really valuable, about which I am absolutely delighted.

Of course there were those in the village who objected. One of whom was John Hodgson, of Kerrol Farm, an incomer who formed The Skye Wind Action Company (SWAG) and tried to stop the whole thing. He was the Conservative candidate (God knows why they selected him!!) and he caused many thousands of wasted hours and money for the Highland Council with his persistent requests for information, fatuous objections and repeating absurd RSPB fears that eagles would be minced up.

One day I received a letter out of the blue, which started "Dear Major Hilleary, As a neighbour, I hope we may let "bygones be bygones". It is rumoured that there have been some cancellations for the Skye Ball this year. I wonder if there is any chance of getting four tickets? Yours sincerely John B.P. Hodgson" I hit the roof, for this fellow had been causing havoc and had been a real problem, so I thought I should be a bit careful in my reply. I wrote, "Dear Mr Hodgson, Thank you for your letter about tickets for the Skye Balls. Tickets are only available through Members and so you should apply through that route. I do not know where you heard the rumour about cancellations, but I fear that is not the case. Yours sincerely, Ruaraidh Hilleary".

Nothing then happened for several weeks until eight of us, including Michael and Bunty Burton hired a lovely big yacht called IKRA 2 belonging to Anthony Haig's cousin, to sail down the Dalmation coast from Split to Dubrovnik with Marigold MacRae, Anthony and Belinda Haig and Brian and Lucy Poett. During the passage, Michael announced that he had been the author of the Hodgson letter; so I had been properly "had"! So knowing of Michael's obsessive hatred of all predators, I then arranged for a letter to be written in Arabic to "Sheik Burton", from another Sheik. It stated there was a great demand for peregrine falcons in this part of the world and asked if he would like to create an eagle and peregrine farm on the Shiel Estate, recently put on the market by the Burton Property Trust. I then got the Lawyer Jonny Wotherspoon, to telephone Michael to say the he was representing a firm of Lawyers in Bristol called Brown, Murray and Peel who had been briefed by the Sheik to offer four million dollars for the Shiel Estate, but that the offer would be a day late for the closing date.

Strutt and Parker were conducting the sale and great excitement prevailed, until Michael checked up on the Bristol firm who of course did not exist; so he telephoned me to say that he thought this letter may have come from Skye. I think we were all square before Michael so sadly died.

When I sailed with Tony Stevenson from Gibraltar to Corunna recently, there were a huge number of wind farms up the Portuguese and Spanish coast, several of which had well over a hundred turbines. They are really very elegant structures moving gently and with no noise. A number of people who want to keep wild areas unspoiled and not see any kind of development have some strength in their argument, but it seems to me that if you allow that principle to govern your thinking, you make it almost impossible for young people who were bought up here and love the place, to have any future.

Quite apart from the local community shareholders' interest in the proceeds, the tiny village of Edinbane now has a completely separate annual income for Community purposes, so my contention is that it is a most valuable asset for a very fragile Highland village and the turbines are not disliked by residents.

***

In the mid-eighties I was driving across to Inverness following a lorry carrying an extraordinary contraption, which I could not identify. I stopped it and asked the driver what it was. He said it was a circular saw and explained that the five circular blades mounted on an axle would produce six logs almost instantly. However, one log had flown off and almost killed him so he was taking the machine to the dump. On his cab door he had painted 'Brian Macgregor, Peat Bog Developer' and he said he was developing a peat bog at Moy estate, where he had about 100 acres. His landlord was The Mackintosh (my father used to say there were only three people you could address the word The, The Pope, The Mackintosh and The Devil).

Brian Macgregor had removed most of the surface heather from his peat bog and with a big tractor, towed a sledge carrying an engine which drove two vertical three feet long, six inch diameter augurs, which went down into the peat and extruded two tubes on to the surface. This seemed a brilliant idea so I asked him to build a machine for me so that I could start cutting peats in Skye. I bought a second hand Zetor 700, four-wheel drive tractor, and Brian built a machine which had a single augur which extruded a single tube of peat on the surface and was attached to the tractor rear drive. The leading edge of the shell that held the augur was sharp enough to cut through the surface and after it had passed through, closed it up again. So it left the surface pretty nearly intact with a hole underground, which tended to fill with water.

This meant that it was best to cut on a slope so that the water would not lie there permanently. We fitted a pendulum cutter bar on the back of the extruder hole to cut the peat into twelve-inch lengths on the surface. Traditionally peats have always been cut as a rectangular block by hand and stacked beside the bog. They needed to be turned once in April because the sun in May and June puts on a skin, which resists the water. Too early and frost destroys the consistency so the peat will not throw the water off. The old crofting families used to gather in late April or early May to help each other. They would finish with a drink and a Ceilidh to celebrate the end of winter.

I got Donald MacNab to drive my machine on hire all around the island. It was very popular and great fun. Later, Bindy Beaton and Peter MacRae drove it and we got to know many townships where they were used to cutting peat by hand. We charged £25 an hour for the machine which produced quite a lot of peat and much more than you could possibly produce by hand.

All was going well until one day I got a call from Lachy Robertson. He was a lovely, rotund figure of a man with a very red face who had started life on a croft in Elgol where he was a schoolmaster before the war. He had ended up commanding the Parachute Regiment as a full colonel and returned to Skye to retire. He was king of Elgol and all the area round about it. He summoned me to come down with my machine but I explained I didn't think I could come to the area as it was very rocky and full of bits and pieces with difficult ground and wet patches. But Lachy was such a character and so persuasive that it was very difficult to resist him.

So we took the tractor to Elgol but its back was broken while Bindy Beaton, was driving it. We had to abandon it and I think it is probably still there. I removed the peat cutter and tried to sell it, but the trouble was that you could not justify the cost of that size of tractor only working for a month or two a year. It needed other purposes for the rest of the time, and I did not want to go contracting on other things. I unsuccessfully tried to hire someone from the East Coast with a big, modern powerful tractor who had finished his spring work early. I think they were put off by the idea of coming to Skye with brand new machinery and were frightened with the way things get treated here.

Alasdair, my son, and I evolved the idea of selling the peat we had in stock as Nessie's Droppings. We said that it was thought that Nessie came over to Skye in the springtime, for traces of her movements could be found on the hill. The natives had collected these droppings and called it peat so now you can send your friends a Nessie Dropping as a present. We sold enough to pay for the packaging, but we eventually ran out of stock.

Brian Macgregor is still in business, but cutting peat was discouraged following comments by Prince Charles. It has more or less all stopped now. We could claim we were helping to drain the area when it was on a slope, but in flat places we certainly were not helping.

At one time a contractor laying the hydro-electric line across the bog from Portree took a big JCB out to dig holes for the poles and the tractor became stuck. It sank into the bog and more or less disappeared. I thought it would be quite an interesting project to rescue it and thought up all sorts of ways to do it. I wanted to buy it from the insurance company and give it to Duncan for his 30th birthday, with the challenge that he had to dig it out. However, Brian Macgregor came along and succeeded. He then bought the tractor and then spent several months and a lot of money recovering it. He got it out in the end, and I suppose he got something out of it, but I think it was much more the challenge to him than the idea of making a profit.

I used to watch the venture and slightly wish I'd had a go. But I was quite glad I didn't. It was much more difficult than it looked. The tractor was probably worth several thousand pounds by the time he had got it up, but I don't suppose it was greatly improved by being underground for the best part of a year.

***

I bought my very first motorbike in Skye from Mike Shaw Stewart for about £5 when I was 16. It was a 250cc. BSA with a gear change on the tank, I used to drive it around the island, and fell off quite a lot. As a result of these accidents both footrests broke off.

With nothing to rest my feet on, my right leg had to go on the horn which was on the front fork and my left leg had to be hitched up over the petrol tank. This was all a bit tricky as I wore a kilt all the time. It became particularly difficult when the exhaust pipe fell off, resulting in flames coming out of the cylinder head - I had to watch out not to get singed.

I once took the motorbike to stalk at Kylerhea and left it in a quarry for the day. It rained heavily all day and when I returned, the bike was absolutely sodden. It wouldn't start, so the only way to get it going was to ride it downhill in neutral and then it started after a bit, but shorted out and I got a very nasty electric shock up my balls. I could not stop the bloody thing which was one of the most agonising things I can remember. Another time I got a wasp up my kilt while heading down to Kinloch to stalk again. That time I fell off the bike into a burn. I remember this every time I pass the spot.

Algy Asprey, of the Bond Street jewellers family, was a somewhat unlikely figure to be riding motorbikes. As a Scots Guards instructor at Pirbright during the war, he taught us to ride around sand dunes and extremely rough ground in a confident fashion. It was a great way to learn. Later on, during the war, I had a 500cc BSA which I once rode to Skye on leave. I took the north route, intending to cross at Stromeferry but as it was a Sunday, there was no ferry. The alternative was to go back to Dingwall, to get onto the south road, but I realised that the railway line went along the side of the loch. I thought I would try to ride beside the track.

I started on one side of the line but after a while I was obstructed by a signal wire. I had to lift the bike over the line onto the other side. I rode along there for a bit, only to find another hazard blocking the route so I had to lift the bloody thing over again. After I had done this two or three times, I was getting pretty fed up, so thought I would try riding along the middle. If you go fast enough, you do not feel the bumps quite so much. All went well until, of course, the inevitable train came round the corner so I am not quite sure who got the biggest fright, the driver or me; he was quite startled but I just managed to get off the line in time and it greatly shortened the journey.

At the end of the war a provisional driving licence could be converted into a full licence and all you needed to do was say what groups you wanted to be able to drive. Provided you had been driving for three years, there was no need to take a test, but as I did not have a motorbike at the time I did not put it on the list.

Many years later - I must have been well over seventy - I wanted a motorbike again, so I had to take a test. Eric Jones of the Uig Brewery was my instructor. We would ride around the primary school in Portree, along with two or three other teenagers. Until then I had never read the Highway Code so I was finally able to discover what all those road signs meant.

On the day of my test the instructor gave me a one-way ear receiver, so that I could hear him, but I couldn't answer back. He followed me in a car telling me to stop beside the Royal Hotel, which has a double yellow line alongside. I thought it was a trick but, as I could not argue with him, I did what he told me to do. To my surprise, I passed and got my licence.

I immediately went off and bought a motorbike – a BMW 750. The longest trip I have done on it was to Wales, to Davina MacLeod's wedding to H. Fetherstonhaugh. I then swapped the bike for an even bigger BMW LT100, with 1000 cc. It was so heavy I couldn't lift it up when I fell off it, which I did once in front of the Co-op in Portree, when trying to turn rather too slowly. I could not lift it so a friendly passer-by had to help me.

I used to wear a fish-farming suit, an all-in-one padded thing, on the bike. It would have kept me afloat if I ever fell into the sea. They are very difficult to get out of, but once inside it is pretty nearly impossible to get cold.

Coming back on the bike from Inverness one winter's day I started out at about 10am on the North route, thinking that the frost would be clear by then. However, the road was still slightly icy around Loch Carron. There was a little sparkle on the grass beside the road, and a couple of twisty bits which had given me a fright, so I had to be careful. Sophie, my daughter-in-law had given me a pair of motorcycling gloves,

My BMW

with a windscreen wiper on each thumb, which was really useful for wiping your hand over the visor and clear the view.

Another winter, I drove to Scalpay for lunch with the Walfords. By the time we finished it was dark and pouring with rain. Riding in the rain with traffic coming against you was very unpleasant. I did not like riding at night. But on a fine day, riding a motorbike is a bit like skiing; you lean around the corners. Great fun.

The Apportionment Battle

Peter Lachy McDonald's father had bought Kerrol Farm on the Edinbane Estate from Great Uncle Kenneth. It was about thirty acres of ground and with it he was allocated one and a half shares in the Common

Grazings. He was also the tenant of a croft so he had another share, taking him up to two and a half shares in the Common Grazings. Under the existing legislation he could go to the Crofters Commission and get his shares in the common grazing apportioned. That means they could be fenced off and used exclusively for that particular tenant. He did this and it amounted to approximately one hundred and thirty acres, which he fenced off. He then came to me and asked if I would sell the area and we agreed the value was about one hundred pounds an acre. Peter offered to pay fifty pounds an acre and that would avoid the claw back.

I went home and scratched my head and reckoned, if the price was fifty pounds an acre, it would be better for me to buy my own land back from Lachy, get a grant, and plant it with trees myself. I consulted Alasdair about this as he might have had to replace the trees in later days if they didn't work. At that point we agreed that we would be better to let Lachy have it.

I went back to him, saying I would sell it to him. Lachy, however, said I had spent so long making up my mind, that he wanted to go to the Land Court, which could settle the value. The chairman of the Land Court, was (Lord) Archie Elliott, the judge who had dealt with the previous tree battle and as well as being a Scots Guardsman, had been an older boy at both Sandroyd and Eton with me. Lachy's solicitor put me on the stand first and said he believed that we were good friends to which I agreed that there was no acrimony involved at all, but that we were asking the Land Court for a value. I put my case adequately, then Lachy put his case equally adequately, and I had no cause to question any of it.

The law is that if the crofter wants to buy his croft, the landlord is obliged to sell it to him and if he wants to buy his common grazing land, he can do so provided it's contiguous to his croft, but in Lachy's case, Kerrol was deemed to be a croft. When six weeks later the judgement came, I had to sell the land for sixteen hundred pounds, just a little more than ten pounds an acre, and pay all the legal expenses, which were six hundred pounds.

Archie Elliott retired soon afterwards and the judge who replaced him gave a judgement in a similar case, in exactly the opposite way, which implies that if we were to reopen the case, we might win it. But I was not prepared to pay any more money to lawyers.

The message that came across loud and clear was that it does not pay to be a crofting landowner. The Land Court, anyway, is notorious for standing up for the crofter, and I was particularly disillusioned after

Archie had given a much more favourable judgement over the tree battle. There were no hard feelings between myself and Lachy who just pulled my leg about it. I was, of course, less pleased.

Lachy died some time later and when I saw his widow Mary, I asked her about selling the land back to me, as she was considering selling it to John Hodgson who had bought Kerrol Farm and was upsetting everyone. Two German Dukes, Karl and Willie von Urach Graf von Wurttemberg who had bought Coishletter (all the land north of Edinbane) for forestry had also offered her £25,000. She offered it to me but I had no intention of paying that sort of money. Alasdair agreed to her price, however, so he bought it back from Mary.

The law allows Edinbane crofters to buy all the Edinbane land if they want to. Sooner or later the community buy out thing is likely to be an issue. Apart from being quite fun, there is absolutely no point in owning croft land.

The rent collection, for example, is a splendid joke. In 1836 the rents from 25 crofts in Edinbane were two hundred and fifty pounds, a lot of money in those days. In 1898 the Napier Commission reduced them to a hundred and twenty pounds, which is where they remained until I raised them by agreement, after we won the wind farm battle, to be more or less in line with the Department rents. They are now about one thousand pounds in total across the 25 crofts on the Edinbane estate per year.

If a crofter wants to buy his croft, the rent is multiplied five times to bring it up to date, and then by 15 to get a figure for the sale price, as a guideline. So I currently charge one price if a tenant wishes to buy a whole croft, which could then be sold almost immediately for about twenty times as much. If the croft is held for five years and then sold, the landlord can claim nothing (but on the other hand, if it is sold within five years, the sale price must be split 50/50 with the landlord).

Today many crofters buy their land: Assynt, Borve, Eigg, Gigha, Knoydart, South Uist, North Harris are all community buy outs and this seems to be the likely future of crofting estates, all paid for with taxpayers money. Whether they can then make the land pay over the long term is debatable. Rich industrialists have previously attempted to make it work and sunk their own private money into these things, but a slightly short sighted view along with a good helping of class prejudice has made that more or less impossible now.

It was very disappointing that the salmon farm did not make money for the crofters in the 1980s. It would have been fun if we had been able to demonstrate that we had converted common grazing land on the hill into common grazing in the sea. I would have liked to have made that gesture. But, because of the way the industry has been taken over by Norway, it was not to be.

I have had an excellent relationship with all the Edinbane tenants, particularly George Campbell, the township clerk, who has been a wonderful representative of all the crofting interests. Yet he has been sensitive to my wishes for the well-being of the whole village. We have had our disagreements inevitably, but overall I believe we do understand each other's points of view and I count him as a very special friend, along with his whole family.

Roddy and Peggie MacFarlane have also been tremendous friends in the Wind Farm Company, the Skye Ski Club as well as in many other respects. I value the fact my father was born in Edinbane and we have faced many different situations as allies because of that.

Afghanistan

I have been the stalker for eight young men to get their first stag, one of whom was Alan Macdonald, grandson of Colonel Jock of Viewfield. When I once enquired what he would like to do in later life, he told me that he would like to work for a charity. So, after serving in The Queen's Own Highlanders he went to work for HALO, a humanitarian landmine clearance charity originally set up by Mad Mitch (Colin Mitchell) and Guy Willoughby. Alan was later appointed to work for the UN Mine Action Service in Afghanistan. He invited me to Kabul in 2008 to see what he was doing.

At the end of my visit I flew back to Dubai on a drug lord's airline, but before leaving, Dr Reza, Alan's delightful boss, sought me out to say how much he appreciated my visit "because nobody comes here to see what we do".

I was much humbled by this admission but assured him I should be thanking *him* for all they showed me. It was all extraordinarily interesting. Our drive through the Salang tunnel, built by the Russians in the 1960s to connect Kabul with northern Afghanistan, was an amazing experience. It is 1.6 miles long, with no lighting, no ventilation and many huge potholes. Going north, one had to avoid the oncoming lorries with their headlights full on who were themselves avoiding the potholes. Consequently one never knew which side of the oncoming lorry one would need to take.

Mine clearing with Alan near Kabul

The number of Afghan children with missing limbs emphasises the tragic consequences of all the land mines that have been laid, with no record of where, by the Mujahadin, the Russians and God knows who else.

Alan took over from Dr Reza eventually and ran the programme as its Director before later moving to Somalia with the UN. I nominated Alan for an OBE in recognition of his incredibly important work. He received this in 2014. I look forward to when he returns to Skye with the family.

The Sporran Hunter

It was early in September
When first I heard it told
Of Ruaraidh and the sporran hunt
A story very old.

On Skye we all were gathered
We'd come from north and south
We'd done The Captain's Caper
And of course the Hamilton House.

The grouse we'd also hunted,
Six brace were shot by noon,
And by the time the walk was done
Two snipe had met their doom.

That night we danced on tireless
Till the beer had all run out.
T'was there I heard the legend
Of the sporran and his rout.

Few came to hunt this fearsome
beast
With gun and trap and hound
And fewer still have lived to tell
Of just what they have found.

Of one such man I now can tell
Who lived in old Portree,
A man renowned in that small town
By the name of Hilleary.

He was often seen about the hills
In kilt, with dog at heel
He knew those hills like no one else,
A sporran hunter he.

There's just one way that's known
to man
To trap this fearsome beast,
There's just one bait that he will take
And on to which he'll feast.

For the sporran is a cannibal,
And when he sees the sight
Of the decoy tied around the waist
He can't resist a bite.

His charge it strikes the Cuillins
His roar makes most men quake,
But the mighty hunter Ruaraidh
Knows no fear and does not shake.

For when the sporran charges
And most would take their flight,
Ruaraidh simply lifts his kilt
And the poor beast dies of fright.

CHAPTER TEN

The Skye Gathering

The Skye Gathering Balls happen over two nights in early September, every year. The event has been going since the late 1800's. There are 50 members, made up from families directly connected to Skye, but their guests often come from far and wide. The ball is actually quite small, with only around 200 people attending. The form is formal highland dress or white tie only, with ladies required to wear long dresses to the floor. It takes place in its own purpose-built hall. My grandfather became secretary of the Skye Gathering in 1922 and my father took over from him in 1924 and was secretary until he died in 1974. I then took over from my father and have been secretary ever since.

Meanwhile, Lord Macdonald's family and the Macdonalds of Viewfield and Redcliff have chaired or served The Gathering more or less consecutively ever since those days.

Hugh Macdonald of Viewfield, currently Treasurer, records that the first known mention of a Portree Ball was a report in the Inverness Courier in 1833, when the new Lord Macdonald (Godfrey, the 20th Chief and 4th Lord) was invited to a day of Highland Games.

The day started with hotly contested rowing events, followed by everyone "repairing to the links", where feats of strength like putting the stone and throwing the hammer were held. At least 60 gentlemen sat down to a sumptuous dinner at Jamiesons Inn, probably MacNab's at the Royal Hotel today.

At ten in the evening the gentlemen repaired to the "Town Hall" where the ladies then joined them and dancing was kept up until five next morning.

Clearly the September Gathering was continued, for in 1868 a rather wonderful poem called "The Bachelors Ball" was written. In the late 1930s Colin Campbell of Kingsburgh, who was joint secretary with my father from 1924 until 1937, said that his grandmother had told him "that there had always been a gathering".

After a suggestion made at the previous year's "Gathering", Donald Macdonald of Tormore, Lord Macdonald's factor, called a meeting on the 5th June 1878 "for the purpose of adopting means for the erection of Assembly Rooms at Portree". The Minute book starts from that date.

In attendance that day were: The Right Honourable Lord Macdonald, EH Wood Esq. of Raasay, John Robertson Esq. of Greshornish (my ancestor), Sherrif Spiers of Portree, Alexander Macdonald Esq. of Portree, Donald Macdonald Esq. of Tormore, Henry Macdonald Esq. of Viewfield, and John Mackinnon Esq. of Mossbank.

A sum of £875 had been promised and it was agreed that a stone and lime building would be best, if funds could be procured to erect such.

Mr Mackenzie, an architect from Isleornsay, suggested the new Assembly Rooms would cost about £1,600 to build - nearly twice what was available. There was a difficulty about raising the loan and paying the interest. Accordingly Lord Macdonald proposed building the rooms, if they remained his property. It would be stipulated in the titles that the other subscribers would appoint trustees who would have the use of the buildings at all times as an Assembly and Ball Room. A committee of three was set up, consisting of Mr Wood of Raasay, Mr A Macdonald of Portree and Mr Macdonald of Skeabost, to agree plans and take this idea forward.

At the subsequent meetings the subscribers did not care for Lord Macdonald taking on the project as his own property. The preferred method was that the subscribers were to draw up an Association on the basis of it being their joint property. £25 shares would be offered to certain persons who, from time to time, might be selected by the committee.

By June 1879 the hall was being built and the loans were guaranteed by Lord Macdonald. The founding subscribers, three of whom were Viewfield brothers, agreed to add half again to their original subscription and despite the loans not being paid off, the committee built the fine billiard room and extension in 1890.

In 1892 Harry Macdonald Viewfield proposed the use of Fancy Hill as a future site for the Gathering Games and there followed some entertaining negotiations with Lord Macdonald's agents, which resulted in the Skye Gathering purchasing the games field and a right of access over the road for a multiple of its value as grazing land. Mr MacKenzie, a butcher, had been wont to keep his animals there before slaughtering them.

The early minutes are a nightmare to read, mostly because many of them were hand written by Hugh Macdonald's great uncle, Alexander, whose writing was "interesting". So much so that a few years ago Hugh was asked to "translate" some of Macdonald and Fraser papers held by the Highland Councils archive service.

For some time after the hall was built, maids and valets were allowed to sit in the gallery and watch the festivities, but this was stopped because they spread scandals.

The outbreak of the Boer war in 1899 put a severe strain on the finances of the Skye Gathering, especially as many of the early loans had not been repaid. As a result the Gathering went into cold storage until 1905.

There were no Balls actually held again until 1907, when there was still a lot of debt, some of it still hanging over from the building of the hall, but the ball of 1908 was said to be a very grand affair and went on over not two, but three nights – apparently because not all of the drink had been consumed.

The great war of 1914 nearly finished the Skye Gathering and by 1918 there was a proposal to wind up the Association and sell the hall. This idea was stopped by Kenneth Macdonald of Tote who was one of the oldest members and Senior Trustee.

In 1920 my grandfather, Major EL Hilleary, Johnny Tote's father, Kenneth Lachlan Macdonald, and my other grandfather Duncan MacLeod of Skeabost, took over the committee and the Gathering took on a new lease of life. They leased the hall and reduced the debt annually, so that by 1931 it was down to an overdraft of £446-4-6d, which was considered very satisfactory.

In1926 the retaining wall fell down in front of the hall, doing some slight damage to the houses on Quay Street. It cost £29 to repair.

Between 1939 and 1946 the hall was requisitioned by the RAF and a claim for dilapidations was put in after the war for £204 and 2/-.

In 1950 the loos were built on either side of the front porch for £750. At the same time the Royal British Legion were offered the lease of the hall for £50 a year.

In 1963 the Gathering bought the Meall House next door for £450. It had fallen into disrepair and had been condemned by "the sanitary". A bank loan of £2,000 was taken out to repair the building.

When Hugh Macdonald took on the role of treasurer in 1991 the Gathering had only just finished paying off interest-free loans given by members, as well as a substantial bank loan after repairs to deal with dry-rot in the building. Less than two years later the wall in front of the hall fell down again and £15,000 was spent within 24 hours on engineers' reports on curtilage, before it was rebuilt at a cost of over £18,000.

Skye has a very long history of military and foreign service so there can be little doubt that Highland Dancing and The Games must have been a feature of island life for many years before the eight original gentlemen of Skye got together to form The Skye Gathering. There are few records from that time, but we do know that George Lowe's band probably played for earlier gatherings before the present hall was built, and that his band included Mrs Logan. In 1936 Mrs Logan was presented with a cheque for £50 by The Skye Gathering "for the 50 years of giving us pleasure", and there has been a direct connection between each subsequent band from those days until Paddy and Libby Shaw today.

It was normal practice for young officers of The Highland Regiments of those days to have to pass the Pipe Major's inspection of their dancing proficiency before they were allowed out to attend private dances elsewhere. The consequence was that the standard of dancing and footwork was very different in those days, in contrast to the practice of what is called "reeling" today.

The Balls today are very much exactly as they always were, although there is a difference in the supper room, because today the supper is served on a stage at one end of the hall, which the British Legion put in when they were tenants. There used to be a wall separating it from the hall, and it was all on one level with the kitchen and a coal burning cooker down in the basement. A member would stand on the door to control the people getting in to supper, but dinner on the stage is much nicer.

Various house parties attending the balls produced the food in the early days and my grandfather's cook, from the White Heather Laundry in London, Mrs Newbutt, would be bought up to Skye to produce the supper, which was carried upstairs in a dumb waiter, which still exists.

Most of the house guests were friends, but unfortunately almost all these houses have been sold or turned into hotels today and the Members of the Skye Gathering mainly go away to work elsewhere, so fewer are resident in Skye. As a result today's Ball parties tend to stay in rented accommodation. That makes the whole flavour rather different.

The music, the catering, the atmosphere and the company remains pretty much as it always was, but events have moved on. Yet I still think the Balls retain their magic.

The Games themselves however, have changed greatly since Admiral Sir Roddy Macdonald extended the Games field and introduced sponsorship and more significant prizes. Where local competition used to be the driving force, competitors now come from further afield. The Games no longer feel quite like they did, but of course they make a great deal more money and bring a much higher standard to the challenges taken on.

The Balls are widely accepted as unchanged because we still have our own home in the shape of the hall, unlike other Gatherings such as the Northern Meeting, whose members today are far too numerous and much less local. It may also help to have a continuous secretary, as opposed to frequent changes, but I believe we have a simple formula that works and so we try not to change anything. Dawn over Portree Bay, after 2 nights of dancing to the music of the Isles as a background, does make for a very special experience.

Skye Gathering to St. Petersburg...

In 2003, for no particular reason, I thought it would be fun to try dancing reels in a Palace in St. Petersburg. I made contact with Adrian Terris who was running Yellow Pages in that beautiful city. He was greatly enthused with the idea and invited me to be Chieftain of the St Petersburg Caledonian Society Ball, which they hold annually in the Astoria Hotel, and of which Adrian was the secretary.

It turned out to be a most amusing evening, although it was clear that the copious quantities of vodka and whisky did make the dancing slightly different from what we normally practiced. However, the hospitality was legendary and so a plan evolved for us to bring 230 Members of The Skye Gathering and their guests, to spend a memorable weekend in St. Petersburg as guests of the Caledonian Society there.

We had agreed amongst ourselves that the cheapest option would not have to cost more than £500 so that we could bring some young people. I chartered a 747 from British Airways, which allowed us offer a very attractive travel price and did a bulk deal with several hotels. Of course there were also more expensive arrangements on offer, which Adrian had taken immense trouble to arrange. There was a special private Kirov Ballet performance in the Winter Palace Theatre, which was really lovely, as well as many other entertainments and opportunities to experience the fantastic beauty of the city. The weekend culminated in an incredible firework display in our honour. It was a most wonderful success. The Northern Meeting and Argyllshire Gatherings have tried to emulate our efforts but not, I think, quite so successfully, so far as I can gather.

One of the local guests was Rod MacLeod of the Moscow Caledonian Society who turned out to be a Dunvegan crofter with a Moscow business and a merchant banking background. A year or so later I received an e-mail from him informing me that President Putin had arranged for a million dollars to be available to back a Tattoo in Red Square, and would I please come as his guest. Of course this was too good an opportunity to miss, so I took Jeannie Stewart-Liddon along with me, and what an amazing show they put on. Rod and two Russians got Mel Jamieson, who runs the Edinburgh Tattoo, to assist, and they organised for seating to be on two sides of Red Square which is huge and very beautiful, with wonderful turrets over an arch in each corner.

I shall never forget the finale which involved 600 musicians from all over the world forming up square, in the centre of Red Square, whereupon 400 pipers, also from all over the world, emerged from smoke which was coming from an arch in one of the opposite corners, marched across Red Square playing The Skye Boat Song. That was enough to raise the hair on the back of one's neck, but having formed up on both sides of the 600 musicians, they stopped.

A single piper then started up Amazing Grace which was taken up by all the rest until there were one thousand players of great Highland music, the likes of which I am never likely to see or hear again.

After it finished, Rod took us to The Kremlin where Putin's number two was presenting trophies to all the bandmasters and pipe majors. I had always thought of the Kremlin as sinister and grey, but it is an extremely beautiful building with really lovely rooms. Among the other guests were Tam Dalyell, the MP, and Sheena's cousin, Angus Hamilton (the then Duke). Tam had been a contemporary of my brother Ewan at Eton, so he knew who I was. He had several Russian generals in tow. I struck up a conversation with one who spoke good English and had rows of medals. I asked him what he thought of all this Scottishness, to which he replied, "If Scotland were managing diplomacy today, I think we would get on well". As we share St Andrew as our Patron Saint and the Saltire, perhaps there is more mileage there? Who knows?

A year or so later we finally managed to persuade Adrian to come over to join us for the Balls with another lady from St. Petersburg. It also happened that The Osiligi Warriors were touring in aid of funds for their Kenya village. When I discovered they were planning to perform in Portree High School at exactly the same time as we were having the Balls, I contacted them and they agreed to attend.

As we were about to start the first Foursome Reel, Alasdair made an announcement about the Gathering having friends from all over the world, so would everybody please make way for the entry; and a naked warrior then crept in, waving his assegai and chanting, which Adrian's lady friend did not see, but could only hear. Very sadly, she thought this was some evil spirit and had a fit, which did rather spoil the entry. But later, when things had calmed down, the warriors joined in the dancing and a hilarious time was had by all.

Extract from the Minutes of The AGM of The Skye Gathering, 26th August 1952

The Honorary Secretary reported that the only Honorary Member of The Skye Gathering, Mr Roger H. Williams of No 11 Wall Street, New York had died in November 1950, and it was unanimously agreed that an expression of sympathy on behalf of The Skye Gathering should be sent to his widow. He read a letter from the late Mr Williams describing his visit to Skye in August 1911, and a suitable extract of his letter is included in the Minutes as a permanent record of his reception by The Skye Gathering on that occasion.

The meeting concluded with a hearty vote of thanks to Mrs Macdonald Redcliff and to Miss Macdonald of Tote for their work with the delightful decoration of the Hall for the Balls in 1950, and a vote of thanks to Major and Miss Macdonald of Tote and to others who played with them for the supper extras on each night, and with votes of thanks to the Chairman and the Honorary Secretary.

Mr Roger H. Williams' letter to Mr Iain Hilleary, referred to in previous Minutes: "The memory of our first experience (August 30/31 1911) is still vivid, perhaps because it was such a surprise. We knew no one at Skye, and our expedition thither was a romantic pilgrimage to unknown shores: We arrived at Portree after a few days at Dunvegan, quite unaware that it was the time of the Games and Balls, and of the recherché character of the latter. In fact when I inquired whether it would be possible for Mrs Williams and me to be admitted to the Ball, merely as observers from the balcony, I innocently supposed it was a semi-public affair, and little realised I was suggesting an intrusion on a very exclusive party.

That your Committee not only forgave the brashness of the request, but graciously went beyond it, was a bit of Scottish Hospitality we will never forget".

Dr. A. D. Mackinnon was the Honorary Secretary at the time and his account of the incident, given in the relaxed post-champagne stage of the Ball, was that the Chairman said: "Archie, what shall we do with this long legged Yankee? He seems a decent chap and his wife is a damned good looking woman! Shall we let them in?"

"Among the dances on the program of the 2nd Ball that year was a new one, the "Two-step", which was as yet, little known in Britain, but as Mrs Williams and I had tried it in New York, we ventured to the floor. Lady Macdonald of The Isles took note – and at her behest we were formally presented and her gracious welcome is still a cherished memory.

This naturally led to acquaintance with a number of the group. Among those of our vintage were your good Father (Major E. L. Hilleary) and one of the Hamiltons. We later learned that of the younger men we met, many shortly thereafter gave their all at Ypres and other early engagements in World War 1. This brought us, as to you, much pride and sadness. I daresay the late War's toll in the Highland Regiments was as great".

Signed: Harry Macdonald. Redcliff. Chairman

**

The Bachelors Ball

There lies an Island in the West
Which exiled natives love the best
And all return to seek a rest
In their dear Island Sgitheannach.

In this dear Isle there lived a band
Of youths who owned both house and
land,
Yet ne'er had plighted heart or land,
But lived as jolly Bachelors.

Their hearts must have been very tough,
For on this Isle there dwelt enough
Of pretty girls who were the stuff
To cheer the hearts of Bachelors.

Now in the autumn----sixty eight
Those youths resolved to give a fete,
When each might lately choose a mate
And be no more a Bachelor.

They sent invites to one and all
To come and grace their Portree Ball.
There all were welcomed, great and small
By those most courteous Bachelors.

They spared no pains to make it gay,
Had Pipers and a Band to play,
And kept it up 'til break of day
Those merry hearted Bachelors.

The room was decked with garlands fine,
And gaudy plaids in varied kind.
As supper good, and choicest wine
Displayed the taste of Bachelors.

MacLeod of Greshornish danced each reel
And footed it neatly, toe and heel.
His handsome dress and stately mien
Proclaimed him Chief of Bachelors.

Doctor Nicol Martin did not dance,
Perhaps he feared to make his chance
Lest some bright eye with killing glance,
Would win him from the Bachelors.

Gallant Captain N.Macleod, from Rhum
(A great loss if he had not come).
And Waternish, who is said by some
To be the Flower of Bachelors.

Messers Humphreys, Scotland, Donald
Tormore
Were often seen upon the floor
And A. Macdonald who had rather more
Than his share of Law, for Bachelors.

Willie MacLeod, with his friend "Glen"
Who think each other the first of men,
Danced very hard like all the Ten
Who make the list of Bachelors.

T'were hard to mention every one
Were I to try, I'd ne'er get done,
But all the guests seemed glad they'd
come
To dance all night with the Bachelors.

There were Lords and Ladies of high
degree
And Commoners, like you and me
T'was truly a pleasant sight to see
The pretty girls dance with Bachelors.

MacLeod and Macdonald in days gone
by
Had 'oft had bloody wars in Skye.
Let ancient feuds forgotten lie,
Nor mar the glee of the Bachelors.

Admiral Sir Roddy Macdonald resigned from the Management Committee, which was a bit of an embarrassment for he was a very splendid man who would have been tremendous as a war leader but in peacetime, he was a great one for administration and tiny details, so he became really tiresome.

Shortly after he arrived in Skye we put him on the Management Committee, and every other day he would ring me up about some slate that was missing or some window that was broken, which was nothing I could do anything about anyway and he just wanted to be helpful. Eventually though, I had to say to him "Look here Roddy, this is becoming a real bore and you are taking it all far too seriously. It is supposed to be fun, running The Gathering". So he said he would resign. I said that was fine, but I think he was slightly taken aback when I took that line.

He then went to Johnny Macdonald who was the chairman, and said that I was finding him very difficult so he offered to resign. Johnny, who was just as bored with all this detail as I was, also said that would be fine so poor old Roddy resigned. To give him his due, he never allowed that to stand in the way of our friendship at all. He was absolutely delightful as a neighbour and a friend ever since, which all goes to show that he was a lot bigger than he might have appeared when he was being a niggling nuisance.

We have always kept the membership at fifty, and there is a waiting list but every single year I would get an attack from Jock McLeod when sailing with him, about why one of his nephews is not a member. I had to tell him each time that the management committee would not agree because he has not got a base on the island. To be a member of the Gathering, people should actually be involved in the life of the island and contribute something, either on the island or somewhere nearby. The Rules stipulate persons resident in Skye or the adjoining mainland. There are probably one or two anachronisms, but on the whole we have stuck to relations of residents.

There was a fellow, who I think became The Earl of Verulam, who came to the Balls without a ticket once. He banged into Sheena in the middle of a reel and she complained about his being rough, so I looked out for him. He probably knew that I was watching him and he disappeared into the loo, dressed in a tailcoat with white facings on his lapels. When he came out of the loo, he had taken the facings off so was clearly trying to change his appearance. However I spotted it, caught up with him and tapped him on the shoulder and asked whose party he was in, to which he replied that he was in so and so's party.

I pointed out that that person had not got a party, and I asked where he had got his ticket from. "Oh," he said. "I bought it in the square." "Right," I said. "You're out." My father was Secretary at the time so we frog-marched him out between us. Later he sent a long letter on frightfully grand paper, full of abject apologies, explaining he was chasing some girlfriend.

We do want to retain the old fashioned elegance of the Balls. I do not think there can be any doubt that the sight of a lady in a long dress dancing gracefully to the music, is a very beautiful sight and a lovely thing to watch, whereas a short skirt really would not look right. Consequently, we do insist on ladies wearing a dress that covers the ankles and men have to wear Highland Dress or a tailcoat with a white tie.

In my youth Mrs Grant had an establishment in Nairn where she taught everybody how to dance by learning the Pas de Bas with their feet, something that is sadly lacking today. Everybody today seems to go, what they call, "reeling", and in my view that is just learning the movements and not dancing the steps. Oh that this could be imparted for it makes the whole wonderful fun of a Highland Ball completely different if the men take the trouble to learn that simple element of what to do with their feet.

In the preface to the Skye Collection of Pipe Music, written in 1898, the author complains about the standard of dancing resembling a railway clog dance. I don't know what a railway clog dance was, but really they were complaining about exactly the same things in 1898 as we do today. So things clearly have not changed a lot. We did have an embarrassment one year when somebody had to be asked to do something about the length of her dress and it was certainly awkward, but hopefully now forgotten.

I have attempted to appear tough about behaviour, out of respect for local feelings. I do not like the sense that we are in some way privileged because we can have a party that is licenced until 6am on a weekday, two nights running. Inevitably this brings the contrast into focus with other local events (who do not get such lenient treatment over licences) and so we must justify that by observing the courtesies punctiliously.

I therefore always insist on jackets remaining on and a strict observance of the rules so that we may continue to enjoy what The

Northern Meeting's original purpose was stated to be as "Pleasure and innocent amusement".

I think it has worked so far. Certainly I find it extraordinary that at six o'clock, or whatever time it is we finish in the morning, very many people leaving to go home, stop and say - thank you, we've had a wonderful evening, we've enjoyed everything and you are quite right to keep the standard up.

The Balls are a delicate subject for they represent landowners and some of the things to which the left-wing element locally, are totally opposed. So when they have finished stirring up tales of the Clearances and all the terrible things that were done, along come the Hooray Henries and dance the night away, theoretically drink too much and stir things up.

Colonel Jock Macdonald, a great local character much loved by everybody, was very keen to get some locals in as members and involve them in the Balls, so we elected three: Douglas Mackenzie, the baker, who is currently still a member, Ewan Mackenzie, who was number two at the Royal Bank, who has since resigned and then died, and Hamish MacIntyre, who was the newsagent, and has also died. But apart from Douglas who came occasionally, they never came to the Balls. No other locals have asked to come.

The whole event has been a great privilege to be involved with. I believe it has been always been a constructive event, that brings good money into the Island. It has certainly brought much pleasure to many people over the years.

From Mrs Emma Mackenzie of Farr.

"Dear Ruaraidh, oh Ruaraidh! I'm on bended knee!
With the reason below I'm quite sure you'll agree
To get rid of five daughters is no easy thing,
They can't sew, they can't cook & they can't even sing....
(like you!)
But the one thing they can do that gives them a chance
Is reel and turn beautifully when at a dance!
Though tickets are "gold dust" we're desperate to buy
To get rid of some daughters while dancing on Skye!!"

'Hogmanay!' by Alasdair

CHAPTER ELEVEN

Sailing

At sea

Sailing has always been my passion. When we came to live in Scotland, Murray Bell, a farmer on the Moray Estate farm of Morayston near Dalcross airport, asked me to join him on his very beautiful yacht, St Kilda, a forty foot Salar motor sailor. Every year we would do a long local trip, or go down to Spain, or over to Sweden and Norway. It was always very good fun. St Kilda was a lovely ketch with a splendid coach house, just aft of midships, and six berths. She was extremely comfortable and Murray took intensive care of the diesel engine which he looked after like his tractors. Ian Mackenzie, a lovely retired Inverness farmer with a large red hooked nose, was Murray's completely unflappable right hand man on the boat. He was always with us.

During one crossing of the North Sea with Murray, I was on night watch. It was raining hard with a big sea running. There was another boat on a converging course and Murray had asked me to let him know immediately if anything exciting happened during my watch. I had seen this boat converging on us quite quickly, but I reckoned I could pass under his stern without any difficulty. As he was getting pretty close, I thought I ought to wake Murray which I did, and he immediately said that I could not do that and told me to jibe at once. So I did; and there was a horrible rending sound as the mainsail ripped from one end to the other. I was not very popular at all.

We were heading for the Gota Canal, which runs right through Sweden into the Baltic from Gothenburg with the entrance to the canal through a huge lock. We called in somewhere south of Gothenburg first, to get the sail repaired before continuing. As we waited to enter the canal, I telephoned my old friends John and Carol Hudson-Davies in Oslo and they came over to join us for dinner; and I don't think Murray appreciated quite how much whisky was needed to see them off the next day.

The trip took about two or three weeks, with Murray organising everything meticulously. He liked to plan where we were going to be at a certain time so that other crew could take over and change places. He had a number of friends who enjoyed his company sailing so we would be about four to six at any one time. Colin Campbell of Balblair, on The Black Isle, shared a cabin with me on that trip. He was enormous fun but pretty outrageous and the only man I have ever met who had been arrested for being drunk in charge of an aeroplane, when he landed one day at Edinburgh Airport. He was a most amusing chap but I think Murray became a bit fed up with him. He had an endless string of rather risqué jokes. He left it in his will that he wished to be buried standing upright, facing the pub, but they couldn't make the hole deep enough.

We crossed the Bay of Biscay en route to Spain one year. I had joined Murray at Cork, having flown down and got a taxi with a driver who had the most enormous stomach with a leather apron sporran thing to stop the steering wheel making a hole in his trousers. He delivered me to the boat where we had drinks and lunch. After lunch we set out straight into the Atlantic where there was a big swell running and I was sick the whole way to Spain. I think the gin and tonic to start with was what set it going, it was dreadful. I do get seasick sometimes, but I usually do get over it.

If there were just two of us sailing, perhaps just Jock MacLeod and myself, it could be hard work. But if there were more than two, it was fine. Sailing with Murray, who always liked to get to a certain place by a certain time, meant little opportunity to explore; but sailing with Jock was different because he liked finding deserted little out of the way places we didn't know were there.

Later sailing was with John and Carol Hudson-Davies, a Grenadier neighbour in Sussex and friend, who was half Norwegian. They had a beautiful 40 foot Halborg Raasay yacht in Lymington and St Malo where his mother, (who had been "Tante Marie" in the Resistance), had a lovely flat.

I remember joining them to see the finish of a race at the mouth of the Oslo Fjord. We anchored in a bay where the finish was expected and had a lovely evening. At 6 o'clock the next morning the winner came by and greeted John with the words: "A terrible thing has happened John. One of my crew has opened a bottle of whisky and thrown away the cork, so, we have to finish it!"

Quite a lot later, returning up the fjord to Oslo, we passed a very beautiful "Colin Archer" yacht anchored en route. Her skipper greeted John and asked us on board. By that time we were pretty well oiled after the race, but our new host insisted on supplying us with Aquavit, the lethal local homemade brew. After this I was convinced that I could walk on water. It became a slight, but not quite lethal, shock, to discover that I could not.

***

Sailing in Trieste while I was based there with the Scots Guards after the war, was probably the warmest sailing I ever did and it is where I really learned to sail. We had a number of Dragon type boats, acquired from the Italians, called Stars. They were very fast yachts, with a crew of two. We had a lot of fun with them and it was customary to have a bottle of Asti Spumante on board so that when somebody sailed close to you, you could fire a cork at them.

Jamie Dunbar Nasmith was a brother Scots Guards officer in charge of sailing at that time. He taught me a lot about how to handle a yacht.

I became part of the central Mediterranean Forces (CMF) sailing team against the British troops in Austria (BTA) team and whenever they came down to sail against us in Trieste, in the Adriatic, we could beat them because we knew the local conditions, whereas when we went up to the Vortesee, in Austria, which was surrounded by big mountains, they could always beat us.

The Bora was a very powerful cold wind that came down to the Adriatic from the Russian Steppes unexpectedly and could easily dismast you if you did not know what you were doing, and very cold it was too. We used to sail round the wreck of the old Rex, a huge liner aground some distance from Trieste, and sometimes Venice opposite.

Although Trieste is where I learnt to sail properly, I had always messed around in boats. During the war General Sir Kenneth and Lady Phoebe McLeod lived at Redcliff in Portree and we used to see a lot of them. Jock McLeod, their son, was my good friend and sailing partner. Their daughter Janet, was my age. When he was growing up, Jock always did what his mother said, was on time and generally well-behaved. Janet and I were beastly to him and rebellious. So much so that Jock refused to go to Eton because I was there ahead of him, so he went to Wellington to become a Regular Seaforth Highlander. In later life Jock teamed up with "Blondie" Hasler, the famous Royal Marine, and they designed a Junk Rig and a self- steering gear together for the wonderful Ron Glas boat that Jock entered for the first Single Handed Transatlantic Race in the '60s. He became known as "Pyjama Jock" because he did not need to get out of his cockpit to change the sails.

Ron Glas had Jock's cabin aft, a very narrow cockpit with a sliding roof and a huge saloon forward with four bunks and Jock's chart table. Built of cold moulded ply, on a cross principle, she was extremely strong, like a lifeboat, and stood up to some tremendous strains.

As Jock's soldiering, and then his adventurism, percolated through to me we became very good friends. We subsequently sailed many a long mile together all over the place. We had one little adventure en route to sailing the whole length of Norway one year, setting out from Inverness through the Caledonian Canal to Plockton, and then up the West Coast to Shetland, to make the hop across the North Sea to Bergen.

As we approached Shetland, the wind was blowing pretty hard, there was a big swell running, and a rock off Sumburgh Head that we knew about. The Clyde Cruising Club instructions said if you kept very close to the shore, you could go between the rock and the shore, which is what we aimed to do as we approached the little harbour where we were going to anchor. But we got it wrong. We hit the rock and got stuck on it. It was about six o'clock in the evening and we both had a dram in our hands. Jock's face went rather green as we hit this thing. The boat heeled over as the wave receded and she started crashing down on her side. Every time the wave rose, we moved further onto the rock and every time the wave receded we thumped back down on the side.

I went up to the bow to try and see what was going on ahead, and was very nearly thrown into the sea by the waves banging her down. It was only a matter of time before she holed and broke up. It was all quite exciting. Jock, rather greener now, had started the engine to try and move her backwards, and of course, she would not move. Then, there was a splintering sound and I thought we were in for a swim. But she came off. The splintering sound was the skeg breaking off. The skeg was a four-inch laminated mahogany post which protruded down behind the keel and on to which the rudder was mounted. Breaking the skeg off freed us from the rock, but the rudder, which was on a two inch bronze shaft, was bent like a hairpin, so of course we couldn't steer. So there we were, with this big sea running, very close to the shore, going round in circles.

Fortunately, someone had been watching what had been going on and a small boat came out from the shore. He asked Jock if he needed a hand and Jock said he would offer a reward, but he would not pay salvage which is apparently the form. If you go abroad and get into trouble, boats coming to the rescue frequently claim salvage if they help you, so the acknowledged form is to deny you want any help. This fellow was genuinely out to help us and I think he must have been rather offended but he threw us a line nevertheless and towed us into the little harbour at Sumburgh.

We then had to decide what to do for we could not move, being unable to steer, so it was quite a problem; but Davy Williamson appeared with the tug boat Zenobia and agreed to tow us up to Lerwick.

Davy was a wonderful character. A short man with a crew cut and Mexican moustache whose standard reply to any question was: "no problem." He would fix anything and go anywhere. The Zenobia was an ex-government, sixty to seventy foot boat, with rubber tyres all around the side. It functioned as a kind of salvage boat. Ron Glas had to stay at the Malakoff Yard for a whole year while she was virtually rebuilt, so we made a lot of friends in Shetland while we watched progress.

Ron Glas at Lerwick

The Klondykers were Russian factory ships that would come in annually to Lerwick, buy the locally caught herring and mackerel, process them on board and then return to Russia via Ullapool and elsewhere. They were all rusty old hulks and pretty scruffy ships. Davy used to order them not to throw their rubbish overboard. He invented the rules I think. One of his little ploys was that they would pay him to collect their rubbish and dispose of it.

There was one commissar who was a real bore apparently, a very difficult chap. At the end of one season after a number of contretemps, Davy and his brother decided they would pull his leg. They got an old music deck, which was broken and let it be known they were going to make a presentation to thank him for all his help, even though he had been a continual bloody nuisance.

They sailed Zenobia up to the boat and the commissar appeared on the bridge. Davy made a little speech of welcome with his tongue firmly in his cheek, and then they handed over the music outfit. Just before the commissar reached for it, they dropped it into the sea. The poor old commissar was frightfully upset as his presentation sank out of sight.

When all the work on Ron Glas was complete we gave Davy a wooden loo seat inscribed with our signatures to thank him for all his help. Two or three years later I was up on the hill behind Skirinish when I saw a Range Rover appear. It was about the time the Skye bridge was being built. I could not think who this could be when a huge man about seven feet tall got out, and sitting beside him was Davy Williamson. They had come to pay me a visit. This huge fellow was a Falkland Islander skipper of one of the boats working on the bridge, and he had made friends with Davy.

It was about four o'clock in the afternoon so I fished out a bottle of whisky. I have never seen a bottle disappear as quickly. Davy was fun. I do not think the Klondyers come to the Shetlands any more as there are less fish and more regulations. They were hugely unsafe.

Once the repairs on Ron Glas were completed, we continued to Bergen the following year. We then sailed the whole length of Norway, via the Inner Leads. It was a fascinating cruise, lasting more than a month.

There was one exciting moment, as we left the shelter of the islands to get round Stadtlandet, the most exposed, westerly point of Norway, open to the full Atlantic gales. We had to head straight into the wind before we could see the marks leading us out and that was quite a hairy moment for one could not turn round, having committed to start out; but fortunately, there was the mark we wanted so there were sighs of relief at having found it.

A cousin of Jock's, John Dent, a great friend, whose family were Skye relations, farmed in Kent. His shepherd, Ross, known as Mr Tiggs, had a small aeroplane in which he attempted to fly John up to join us at Bodo. They had bad weather trying to cross the North Sea from Aberdeenshire, so had to go all the way back south to Kent in order to cross over and then fly north. John and I then exchanged places and I flew back with Ross in a very hairy and bumpy trip down the fjords to Stavanger from where we eventually managed to cross back to Aberdeen. As we approached the land, and running very short of fuel, we had to dodge an extremely nasty looking black thunderstorm just as we succeeded in landing.

***

Just after the war I used to sail in a lovely boat called Gladeye, which belonged to the Brigade of Guards Yacht Club at Warsash on the river Hamble in Hampshire. She was one of three very beautiful 100 square metre yachts that had been requisitioned from Germany after the war. She belonged to The Royal Marines, The Gunners and The Rifle Brigade. Gladeye originally had the German name of Eis Vogel, but was rechristened after The Ever Open Eye, which was the divisional sign of the Guards Armoured Division in Germany.

She was a sloop with beautiful lines, but no engine. She had a permanent skipper called Diaper in charge. Diaper's father had been skipper of one of the old J- Class boats, which were the biggest yachts ever built between the wars. They needed a huge crew and were really beautiful old classics.

We sailed on Gladeye many times. On one occasion, we were going over to the Isle of Wight with Bill Lawson, who was extremely proud to have just been elected to the Royal Yacht Squadron - the only club allowed to fly a White Ensign except for the Royal Navy. The crew consisted of Colin Dalrymple, Adrian Seymour and a couple of others. We knew that there was a sandbank opposite The Squadron but managed to get stuck on it. I started laughing, so got a bollocking and was told to pull myself together and throw a kedge off the stern, which I did; but the kedge got hooked on to the trotts, which are the permanent anchor lines on the bottom. We managed to get off the sand bank, but we could not get the anchor up and were going round in circles. Poor old Bill, right in front of the Royal Yacht Squadron was getting more and more embarrassed. It was rather unkind to laugh at him I suppose.

We had a lot of fun with Gladeye. We won the Round the Island race once. Years and years later, like about ten years ago, I was driving in Inverness beside the canal, when I saw on the shore, a very beautiful looking hull. It was out of the water with no mast, and being worked on. I stopped to have a look and said to the old man working on it that it was a beautiful looking boat that reminded me very much of a boat I used to sail called Gladeye, and he said that this was Gladeye. He had bought her, and renamed her with the original German Eis Vogel, converted her to a ketch and given her an engine. It was such fun to meet up with her once more.

Ron Glas, which is the Gaelic for grey seal, has been aground once or twice. Jock calls it "the overland route", which we are not really supposed to take. A year or so ago the transom - which is the back end of the boat

- was delaminating and he had to have it rebuilt, so we delayed the start of our planned cruise, while the work was carried out at the Caley Marina in Inverness. To start off we had to sail through the canal down to Loch Linnhe and on.

As we left the canal into Loch Linnhe, against the wind and the tide, we needed the engine to get clear of all the junk at the head of the loch. It was running slightly faster than normal, and started overheating. We decided to return to the sea lock in the canal to see what was wrong. An engineer from the yard then announced that we had a cracked cylinder head and had to go back to Inverness.

We tacked all the way back up Loch Ness. At six o'clock in the evening, when things start to look a bit more cheerful, we were studying the Gaelic label on a bottle of whisky, when there was a horrible grinding sound, and we went aground just opposite Castle Urquhart.

This was a bit undignified as Ron Glas is quite well known with her Junk rig, and here was the famous Jock McLeod, as he liked to be called, the single handed trans-Atlantic sailor, aground. We got the dinghy out and dropped the anchor well out and so got her going once more on the opposite tack towards the Clansman Hotel. The next thing we knew we had done it again a second time.

That was the end of the cruise. We were just not paying attention, talking too much. I have never seen the Loch Ness monster but I am quite certain there is one.

I sailed with Jock all over the west coast from his winter base at the Caley Marina in the Caledonian Canal, which had the advantage of fresh water and consequently prevented barnacles. The first base for the summer cruise was always Plockton where he had Murray Bell's old mooring and could leave the dinghy in the garden of Theresa Peach's lovely house at the old pier. From there we would sail round all the Islands. He knew of so many wonderful deserted anchorages that we could visit after a hard day. A dram and a brew up in such circumstances are the epitome of West Coast sailing and must surely be the best area in the whole world to cruise.

We found several rocks, some of which are perfectly well marked, but Ron Glas stood up to our ravages brilliantly. On one occasion coming out of the shelter of Drumbuie, a beautiful anchorage just opposite Tobermory, and heading north on a windless morning, we banged into Sliganach Beag which was covered. We were both standing in the cockpit when we hit the rock and so two very bloody noses resulted. As we limped into Tobermory, the lifeboat helped us in. They must have thought we had been fighting!

Another time sailing with Jock, we called in at Arisaig to pick up Jacky and Vora Shaw Stewart. We crossed over to Eigg with a view to calling on Fergus Gowans - the County Councillor for Eigg. Fergus's parents, Robin and Violet stayed at The Cottage in Dunvegan during the war - Robin had had a German Eagle tattooed on his back. They had a weedy daughter, rather like Popeye's Olive Oyl, called Josephine, and Fergus was even skinnier. After Robin and Violet died, Fergus became the local Councillor, and took to the bottle, making quite a reputation for himself as an alcoholic on Eigg. I had not seen Fergus since he was a little boy, so thought it would be fun to call on him at his house up the hill.

We landed and walked up to find Fergus. He remembered me, so we went in and had a dram. He was in fine form, and I believe he must have had a wife. In due course it was time to leave and we found the Eigg taxi waiting for us. It was a large Landover with an enormous rope holding the bonnet down, no number plates or anything like that, and a rather splendid looking driver. He had waited because anyone calling on Fergus Gowans would almost certainly need the taxi.

We really didn't think there was much option but to get in and use him. I got in the front and made a few remarks to the driver who took a longer look at me and said that he thought he knew my face. I took another look at him and said that I thought I knew him. It turned out that he had been a crew member of the Loch Nevis, the steamer, which used to ply between Mallaig, Kyle and Portree during the war. He was quite a figure on the boat, and seemed to remember me from which point onwards he did not look at the road at all. He concentrated solely on me. The steering wheel was completely worn out and had to be turned several times before it had any effect, so it was the hairiest drive I think I ever had.

***

In the late 1960's I was running the boat yard at Findhorn for Arthur Munro Ferguson and bought a delightful little 28-foot bilge keel yacht called Serendipity, in partnership with David Erskine, Arthur's Factor. He did not use her very much at all so I took her through to Skye and we had some lovely sailing all round the islands. My son Alasdair and I sailed Serendipity from Arisaig to the Shaw Stewarts at Traigh one evening, aiming to leave Traigh at eight o'clock to sail round the north end of Skye through the night to Tayinloan.

As we passed the point of Sleat and came up beside Rhum, the light on the point of Sleat disappeared over the horizon. At the same time the Heiskeir light between Rhum and Canna was hidden behind Canna, and the moon went behind a cloud. It was complete darkness. I was on watch and steering, while Alasdair was below having a kip. It was about midnight. There were no lights anywhere, but we had set a course for the night in order to arrive at Neist point in the morning. I suddenly experienced a prickly feeling up the back of my neck that there was something ahead.

I could not make it out, so I woke Alasdair to check the navigation and our course. He agreed it was correct. I said I thought it had to be Rhum or Canna ahead, although I couldn't see how; so I decided to turn off to starboard and hope for the best. If it was Soay, which was opposite and on our right side, we would bump into Skye. We clearly had to make a choice but still could not see, so we turned right and after a bit the compass came right back again, and we were back on course.

What had happened was that we had got a bit close to Canna's magnetic Compass Hill. It pulled the compass right off course. It was the most extraordinary experience which taught me always to read the small print on the chart and discover when there was a magnetic anomaly.

Ian Campbell, the stalker at Eileanreach, later told me exactly the same thing happened to him when he was putting a road in on Eileanreach. He took a bearing to set the road in one direction. Then he went to the other end to take a back bearing to get the two roads to meet. They were way off - there would have been a kink in the road had he not realised that there was a magnetic anomaly in the hills.

Tom McLean was a character I was slightly embroiled with. He had been in 22 SAS with Rod Stewart-Liddon and Chay Blyth. He decided to row, and then sail, the Atlantic in a boat only nine foot six inches long. This was considered quite a feat. A Frenchman then sailed the Atlantic in a slightly smaller boat than Tom's not long after he'd done it. So Tom decided to take a chain saw to the back of this boat and took two feet off, making it seven foot six long and then he did it again!

Today you can go up to the head of Loch Nevis, where he has an adventure school and the two feet off the back of his boat is stuck on the end of his shed, which is beside the boat he did it in. I don't think the Frenchman tried it after that because seven foot six is not much longer than a bath. I saw him after this and asked him how he'd got on with food and so forth. "Ach", he said, he had filled his boat with food, and "just ate my way down".

The other thing Tom did was to claim the island of Rockall for Britain. A television company was going to pay him six thousand pounds to film him doing it. He got a boat to take him out from which they studied the rock and decided that every seventh wave would rise to a certain height, which would allow Tom to get off the boat and onto a ledge. From there he planned to climb the rest of the cliff with ropes and pitons and so on, which were all lashed around his tummy. In due course the timing was set and he drove the boat up to the rock face, and stepped out. Unfortunately the next wave knocked him off. And he went to the bottom, very quickly, with all this stuff around his tummy.

It took him two minutes before he came back up again, full of water, of course. They held him upside down, and pumped him out. Half an hour later he did it again and got up and sat on Rockall for six weeks.

I met him on a Queenie (small scallops)farming course, which we did at Ardtoe at the Seafood Industry Research Establishment. I had come across him once or twice before, and saw quite a bit of him on the course. He was terribly funny. Every time some scientist would get up and give him a lot of information about Queenies and so forth, Tom would say - 'that's a load of balls and completely unnecessary'. This would puncture the poor man completely. Then he would explain what he had done, or would do.

I think he subsequently sailed the Atlantic in a bottle, which he had fitted out with a four poster bed. His nickname is Moby. His latest enterprise is even more interesting. He had a steel whale built by William Reid of Forres, and the last time I saw him he was trying to sell places on this contraption. I think they were six thousand quid a place, to sail the Atlantic in a whale. He does make quite a lot of money with these enterprises.

I chose to attend the Seafood Industry Research Establishment out of interest. Queenies were an interesting shellfish for which there was a good market, and it seemed like they could be grown quite easily. I was rather interested to find out about it and after I'd written to them, they invited me on a course. They did all sorts of research into lobster and cod breeding and were trying to breed whacking great 100-pound halibut which were pretty vicious at that time. If you put your finger in the tank they would have it off. Halibut farming is now an established industry.

***

Another great sailing friend was Tony Stevenson whom I had known at Eton. Not only was he a very good boxer but also considered to be fairly troublesome. I did not really appreciate our mutual tendencies in that direction until I got to know him in the 3rd Battalion Scots Guards just after the war.

Tony had sailed Gladeye across from her home port of Kiel (from where she had been acquired as war reparations) and dismasted her en route. Our paths crossed again when his father installed him in C.E. Heath's, just when I was starting there. However, he had the great advantage of some excellent accounts which enabled him to set up independently in Edinburgh, and so we did not really get together much until a few years later.

Tony had been elected to The Royal Yacht Squadron with a splendid 70 foot converted fishing boat, Jesmond. It was a really comfortable home for some great adventures. We did many west coast cruises from Cruibh Haven, where she had a berth, and after a refit in Fort William we sailed her down to Gibraltar, to a berth at Soto Grande. One very challenging cruise to the Balearics in a gale set Tony thinking that it might be time to stop, but he held on and some time later he and I did a pottering cruise up the Portuguese coast, with his long time, faithful crew, John Nichols.

I was reading a book below when Tony slowed the engine down to indicate we were approaching Cadiz and had found our waypoint, just short of the entrance. I went up on the bridge to find Tony saying to John, "we must find the first mark of the harbour entrance line"; but the sun was going down in that direction and there were a number of boats about so it was very difficult to spot the mark we wanted. I could see a green buoy dead ahead so reported this to Tony who thought it must be the one; but unfortunately it was the second buoy of the line and we went aground, hard.

Tony slammed the engine into reverse, but it was no good and we were firmly stuck on a falling tide, Eventually, as she heeled over, a wave knocked her over to the other side and she must have cracked a rib; for the big lifeboat came out and insisted in our leaving the ship, arguing it was impossible to stay on board. We all thought she would be all right when the tide came back, but as it rose in the dark, we could see that she was filling up and so we had to accept that it was to be her end. A very sad moment indeed for she was a lovely old girl with many happy miles behind her.

With Tony Stevenson on Jesmond

In the morning we had to go and see the Harbour Master. He was very concerned that we had only recently filled up with 7000 litres of diesel in Gibraltar, which could pollute the harbour. He turned out to be one Jamie (pronounced "Heime") Macpherson, the fifth generation of Harbour Master in Cadiz, so I asked him if he knew his Chief. "Yes" he said, "I have just been staying with him in Blairgowrie". That broke the ice for Billy (as I knew him) Macpherson and I had joined the Scots Guards together. We were invited to inspect the original Harbour Master's office, at the back of the current more modern one, where all the old charts from Drake's days were displayed, together with many fascinating relics.

Of particular interest was a glass topped wooden door with a bullet hole in the bottom. It was opposite a bookcase in which there was a book with Drake's bullet still embedded in it. A fascinating bit of history and some new friends were thus, very sadly, the swansong of my sailing days.

CHAPTER TWELVE

Skiing, Cresta and Snow Holes

I started skiing in 1936 when my Mother took me to St Moritz. We stayed at Suvretta House, a five star hotel in the village, and I made friends with one of the waiters with whom we practiced ski jumping on a homemade jump. What fun that was. But even more fascinating was watching the Cresta.

Jim Lawrence and Billy Fiske were the two huge figures of the Cresta at that time, but I was too young to be allowed to try it, even though I did ask. Jim Lawrence crashed at Shuttlecock one morning and broke a rib, but rode again the next morning and broke two more. What really intrigued me was that he rode again the following morning with three broken ribs and I thought that was an example that I would remember with respect.

I did not have the opportunity to try skiing again until I was stationed in Trieste after the war, and Cortina d 'Ampezzo was just a few hours away, in the Dolomites. After that I skied whenever I could, with family and friends.

***

In 1951, the year before I married Sheena, she had invited me to join her ski party. She had arranged it in order to go free herself, before captaining The British Ladies Olympic Ski Team. If 15 people travelled together there would be one free place. We then adopted the principle when our own family started to develop.

Practically every year thereafter we used to take a large party to enable the family to travel free.

Christopher Mackintosh had a so-called "secretary", whose husband David Ross had a travel agency, Lairdways. David once suggested

Macunaga in Italy as the place for us to try, but that was a disaster, with holes in the walls between the bedrooms and dreadful skiing.

On the way back home from that trip, three members of the party got out of the train in their pyjamas to buy wurst at Stuttgart station, just before we got to the Belgian frontier. Then the train pulled out without them, leaving them standing on the platform.

Jamie Dunbar Nasmith's brother, Admiral David was with us and he woke me up to explain that Nicholas Bullough, James Hughes Hallett and James Willis had been left behind. So I made up a package of their passports and some money, with a bit of paper to show that they were on a group ticket, and left it at the next station with word that we had lost them, which was really all we could do.

They, on the other hand, decided to use their initiative. They decided they could not stand there in their pyjamas, so they caught the next train that passed through and landed up in Cologne, where they went to the zoo, still wearing their pyjamas. They finally got home in a very splendid effort, in spite of the fact that there was a Willis of the same name, wanted by Interpol for murder. So when they went into the police station for help, they were arrested and locked up!

Another ski party we organised was at Selva, in the Val Gardena. A notice went up in the hotel where we were staying, to the effect that there was to be a race for Alpini soldiers during the time we were there. Someone discovered that I had done some training with the Alpini, so my name was put down on the list of entries without telling me. On the morning of the race the Alpini band came and struck up underneath my bedroom window with wonderful big oomph pah pah instruments and huge moustaches. Their playing woke me, and everyone else, up. I stuck my head out of the window to be greeted that they would see me at the race - something that I knew absolutely nothing about.

I was dragged up to the race, and we were all issued with a number, based on our age. The Alpini were lovely really good mountain people, and damned good soldiers. The oldest member was a General with a huge white moustache, which went literally sideways - and was about 80. He was number one and I came somewhere around the middle. I managed to get to the bottom without falling, followed by great celebrations, barrels of wine and lots of chit chat, so I had my glass of wine, said my thanks and set off. They then said they would see me at the prize giving that evening.

I said "No no, I would not be coming", but they insisted, so that evening, I thought I had better go along and see what they were up to. I was called up to receive a prize, although all I had done was get to the bottom without falling, and my time had been hopeless. However, I was presented with a huge great cup for being the only British entry!

On the flight home the Selva Cup, as it was called, was passed around the party and everyone put a different drink into it. Of course, it was absolutely revolting, but Jeremy Phillips, who was with us, drank most of the mixture and got absolutely plastered. He had bought a very expensive telescopic lens at Munich Airport and so in a drunken stupor, he went through Something to Declare. He breathed all over the Customs people that he had this very expensive piece of kit to which they said "There there, that's quite all right", and let him straight through! It was the most wonderful double take I had ever seen.

We had a ski party in the springtime pretty well every year. One year in Wengen everyone had to have a photograph for their *abonnements* (ski passes). Before we got on the train to Scheidegg, I instructed everyone to change *abonnements,* so when the ticket collector came along men had photographs of women and vice versa. The collector soon began to realise that he was having his leg pulled and got very cross, at which point I got my cine film camera out, and I have this wonderful film of the Swiss ticket collector getting absolutely furious and charging at me, while I was filming him.

One year I answered an advertisement in the Times for a chalet to let in Villars, at a week's notice, belonging to the Lothians. There, whenever there was a queue, one particular individual invariably landed at the head of it. He had a trilby hat and whiskers, and never, ever waited in a queue. Eventually, having watched him going straight to the front of the queue a few times, I tapped him on the shoulder one day and asked him how the hell he did it. He said that he had cancer and was going to die, so could not see any point in queuing. He was Richard Mead Fetherstonhaugh who did indeed die later, but not before he had had an awful lot of fun not queuing. He owned Uppark, in Hampshire, which belongs to the National Trust now and was full of priceless furniture, but sadly burnt down a few years ago. I was very fond of his widow, Jean. Sheena got quite cross about that.

***

In the spring of 1967 we did the Haute Route as an SAS winter warfare exercise. It is normally done from Chamonix to Saas Fe, but we did it in reverse from Saas Fe, sleeping in the various huts en route and carrying all our food. It normally takes about ten days to complete, depending on the weather and you do not drop down much below 10,000 feet all the way.

Haute Route 1967

There were five of us, Roger Wellesley Smith, Bernard Dewe Mathews, Patrick Agnew and Ben Holt, all of whom had done quite a lot of winter warfare training, some with the Alpini in Italy, so we all knew about the threats from crevasses and how to survive in snowholes etc. So we decided not to have a guide for the trip.

We started from Saas Fe and climbed up the glacier to the Britannia hut, then dropped down into Zermatt off two more glaciers. We were coming down the first glacier from the Britannia hut into Zermatt. I forget the name of the first glacier, bit it joins the Findeln. Where the two meet, there is a sort of T-junction of glaciers and I was roped up with Roger Wellesley-Smith. He stopped suddenly and shouted at me to sit down and belay him. I said: 'No. If it is going to avalanche, we should move back gently.' But he kept on repeating it and I realised then that he was standing on a crevasse that had opened up beneath him. So I sat down and belayed him on the rope. The front of his skis were on one side of the crevasse and the backs on the other side, so he was standing on about four hundred feet of nothing and not very happy at all. I managed to pull him in, but he could very easily have pulled me in with him. We were OK in the end, but we decided to take a guide for the remainder of the trip. There was a lot of trouble getting off the first glacier, because the spring conditions meant much avalanche danger and when we got down into Zermatt eventually, completely dehydrated, I remember thinking I had never drunk so much in all my life. You do not drink the snow, because it acts as a filter and brings all sorts of nasties down with it, so is a recipe for trouble.

The Vignettes Hut is one of the stopping places on the Haute Route. To go to the loo there, you have to climb along a ledge and sit on the throne right up on the cliff edge, with a thousand feet below you. You could see choughs circling below and aim at them, although it was pretty draughty. It was all very arduous skiing, with much of the snow breakable wind crust. With a heavy pack on your back, one had to be very careful.

One night we shared the hut with a German party. The next morning our guide said they thought they were going to beat us so he suggested we take the shorter route out, which meant that he led us up an absolute precipice, so steep that I would have thought it was almost not safe. We were doing kick turns, and were roped, but it was very difficult to belay anyone there, and had we fallen, we would have fallen a very long way. I did not enjoy that climb but we beat the German party.

When we got to the Grand Combin, it was avalanching, so we had to divert from the conventional finish and complete the trip in Verbier.

The whole thing covered the best part of a hundred miles, and we were snowed in for a couple of days in one of the huts.

***

The Shuttlecock Club at the Cresta was started by my uncle, Angus MacLeod, and it continues to this day. A novice rider has to start at Junction after which there is a long straight ending with the right handed turn of Battledore and immediately after that, the left-handed Shuttlecock. If you get round Shuttlecock successfully, all brakes are off, rise is a gentle right hander and then a straight with Cresta Leap, Scilla and Charybdis, ending with a slight rise and the absolute delight of the finish at which point the rider may be nudging 80 mph.

One could only become a member after crashing at Shuttlecock, which is a long left handed turn with banking that is only just high enough to negotiate, provided that you come out of the right handed Battledore at the right angle.

I had an opportunity to do my first Cresta run when I was 54. Apparently I made quite an impression with my first ride because I did a very good time. Faster in fact, than any man over 50 had done on his first ride. This was possibly because I had remembered each detail from childhood. As I gained more confidence after about three or four runs, I stopped braking altogether, and reached the maximum speed I thought I was capable of.

I got a but more serious next time I went, became a member and persuaded my sons, Alastair and Duncan to come out with me. But I have never ridden from Top. Digby Willoughby was the club Secretary, and running it very well in fact, but he would not let anyone go from Top until they have achieved 47 seconds fairly regularly from Junction. Sadly I simply couldn't get that time.

***

We were skiing in Zermatt once when Sheena and I climbed the Theodul Pass with a cousin, Lavinia Rosenthal. On the top Sheena got frostbitten, so rather than come all the way back into Zermatt, we decided to cross over to Cervinia which was quite close. We found a hotel and discovered the Italian bob team was practising for the world championships. I thought it would be quite fun to have a go on the bob, so asked one of the team if I could have a run. He said no. No. No way. But I persisted, and he told me to talk to the trainer. I found the trainer and he pointed to me and said - wasn't I the man who'd broken his bob in Cortina?

In Cortina, a number of years before, one night after dinner, we'd borrowed Sisto Gillarducci's bob. It was a six man bob. We'd had a system of signals to allow for traffic coming up the road, and the signal was that, when a car came through, we could go. What we hadn't allowed for was two cars coming up, and the second car - remember this was after dinner in the dark - had got stuck. We were coming down the road at Pocol which had a lot of hairpin bends on it, and we were going flat out with myself driving, Peter Balfour on the brake, Colin Dalrymple, Adrian Seymour and two others, rifle brigade people I think. There was just enough room to get through between the car and the bank, it was a Packard I think, and I misjudged it slightly. We touched the bank, hit the side of the car, peeled off the mudguards and I think one of the doors, and the bob went flying off in the trees, and we all got thrown off. No one got hurt, surprisingly enough, I suppose we were all worse for wear after dinner. But the bob got slightly bent.

So when I found this character training the team for the World Championships, we had a good laugh about what had happened to his bob years before. I asked him if I could have a run the next day and he said certainly. He told me to turn up the next day and he'd take me down. So I went along the next morning and he explained what to do. He said he would drive and I was to run like hell and jump on when the thing got started. I was to lean with him around the corners, and if he shouted "freno" I had to pull on the brakes. These were a handle at the back. When he shouted "freno", I had to let go of the handle and grab hold of the brakes.

We started going down, and got faster and faster, and there's a hell of a G when you come into the corner and all the blood leaves your head. We were about three-quarters of the way down and he got it slightly wrong on one of the corners and started shouting "freno". But I couldn't let go of the bob! I was shit scared, and literally couldn't let go. So we didn't touch the brakes at all, but went all the way without them. And we did the second best time of the morning. But it was sheer green terror on my part.

***

Keith Schellenberg who used to own the Isle of Eigg was a great bob man as well as a Cresta rider. However, he managed to have himself kicked out of St.Moritz for getting dressed up as a Swiss Policeman and causing gridlock with the traffic. He then went round asking if anybody had seen a "mad Brit pretending to be a Swiss Policeman". So he founded the Les Avants Tobogganing Club, of which he made me an Honorary President, along with several other reprobates.

In 1994, we went tobogganing in the Tatras in the Czech Republic, with Keith's son Nick in a Land Rover pulling a trailer with four large bob sleighs and 25 luges, which are very heavy metal toboggans. You go down feet first on a luge and all you can see is your tummy, so just hope for the best. We had an amusing trip out as we stopped off at Nick's girlfriend's place in Erfurt, a very beautiful East German town that was being restored with West German money. She was studying to be an architect so after dinner we walked around the town looking at all the lovely old buildings there.

We planned to go through Poland as I wanted to see Krakow and come into Slovakia through the Tatra Mountains. However, when we got to the Polish frontier, customs asked what we had on the trailer. They told us we were transporting a commercial load and we did not qualify to go across the border as tourists. The lorry queue was very long. No one seemed to be paying much attention so I strode into the office and asked in a loud voice if anyone spoke English.

Eventually a little, fat lady emerged and said she would help. She asked how much the toboggans were worth, so we said about two thousand pounds. We were told we could go through, but we had to pay that sum which we would get back when we left. To hell with that, we thought and decided not to go through Poland, so we went all the way back through the Czech Republic and then down to the Tatras, which was absolutely beautiful. We spent a very amusing week. We tobogganed and skied, played ice hockey and ice cricket, which is the sort of cricket where the bowler would arrive before the ball.

Keith had divided us into teams, each of which had an absurd sort of name like the Holy Roman Empire, the Hottentots, the Highlanders or whatever. One then had to dress up in outfits to suit the name with a total mix of the sexes. Peter de la Billiere's daughter was one of the contenders, as was Neil Laughton whose skates I borrowed to join the ice hockey.

The Grand Old Duke Of York was another game which involved running uphill with a toboggan to a start point, where you would then have to come down as fast as possible. Nobody broke anything much I don't think, but there were quite a lot of injuries.

The skiing was in a lovely former East German village called Levoca, with a beautiful old town hall. Keith had collected about a hundred interesting people from all over the world, who were all doing something different, and all out for a different kind of holiday, which Keith was brilliant at organising.

The village mayor gave us a civic reception in the town hall, with a hundred glasses of vodka set out on a huge round table. He then made a welcome speech and Keith gave a splendid reply that here were we, British sportsmen, all up for amateur sport, and this was what he wished to endorse. There followed a demonstration of the local dancing which was very similar to our Highland variety and absolutely lovely, with the local costumes and girls of all ages.

I was tempted to write to the West Highland Free Press saying that I had just come back from a week in Czechoslovakia with Keith and how proud I was to be part of the Schellenberg party who had represented amateur sport in a very splendid and professional way. Keith had come in for a lot of criticism in that newspaper, for what he was, or rather wasn't, doing on Eigg, somewhat unfairly I thought.

The year before I had joined the Skye Ski Club and we went to Bulgaria. We stayed in a hotel which appeared to have been designed like the Tower of Babel. It was a relic of communism and had a thousand beds. There were several dining rooms which each attracted different nationalities such as German, French etc. We were about the only Brits there.

***

The most difficult journey I have ever done was in the far north of Norway. We were to test the security of Bardufoss, the most northerly Nato airfield by parachuting in some way away. We were dropped by the Americans from a C119, but they got lost and dropped us 40 miles off course, up the wrong fjord from where we were supposed to be. I was number one in the aircraft, jumping first, with a sixty-pound pack, a parachute, and a weapon. I had to stand in the door, waiting, while the pilot circled around trying to find out where he was.

Eventually he let us go in the wrong place. It was night so we had to cross forty miles of Arctic tundra carrying a heavy load in the dark. The North Star is bang overhead when you are up there, making it extremely difficult to navigate. It was very tricky.

Anyone who says jumping out of an aeroplane with a parachute is not frightening, is either a liar or very stupid. We did quite a lot of winter training in Norway including about a fortnight in snow holes. You need to find a bank of snow with some depth to it, and then go in, up, and in. Having done that, and made a rounded ceiling, moisture condenses on the roof and runs down the sides. If you do not make it reasonably smooth, it will drip. It is also vital to make a hole up through the roof with a ski stick, so that further snowfalls do not block it, otherwise you will suffocate. A two-man hole is probably the best, for once you get it warm, you can get your clothes off and dry out - body heat does the work. The secret is to make the entrance hole lower than the bed height. It will take about three hours to build and even though it may be well below freezing when you are building it (and you really need a better tool than a ski), you really will warm up. If you can find them, a few branches and twigs make the bed, so that the air can circulate under you.

We had rations, but we augmented them with anything we could catch, mostly fish which we caught through iceholes. One could also trap rabbits or hares, or even Ruiper (which is very like a Ptarmigan, and which turns white in the winter). I have never shot ptarmigan, and I don't think I want to. I remember I was once teaching some soldiers how to make a snow hole in the Cairngorms and ptarmigan came looking in through the hole, as if to say 'What are you doing there?' They were not at all frightened by us and are lovely, beautiful birds.

On another occasion in the Cairngorms, the wind was blowing quite hard, so the ski lifts were all closed. However, I spotted someone parachuting up the hill, so I waited until he came down, and discovered that it was Jamie Dunbar-Nasmith, of all people. He offered me his spare parachute which was a kit-bag type and much smaller than a normal big one.

The form was you put your ski sticks through the rigging lines and let the canopy develop while you hang on to your ski sticks. The trouble is, you can't see anything in front of you and so you just have to hope for the best. If you come across some rocks, you have to move pretty quickly to get out of the way.

I was flying five or six hundred feet from the top of Corrie Cas, across the traverse, to the top of the White Lady and largely avoided the rocks, but when I got to the top, I did not see a man who was bending down doing his boots up. He became rolled up in the canopy and was not very amused. I was extremely apologetic and tried to help him out of the rigging lines, but he was in rather a bad temper. I finally got him clear, when two minutes later, up came Jamie and got him again...

***

Skiing with Sheena at Wengen one year we bumped into Max Aitken. He had a guide, Steger Fritz, with him. We had another guide and were planning to climb up the Mannlichen which did not have a lift at that time, in order to get some spring snow on the run down to Grindlewald. It was quite a long climb and I think Steger Fritz led, with instructions to follow exactly where he led. It was really lovely virgin spring snow everywhere and absolutely wonderful, but I did not turn as I should have, quite where the guide had turned, and of course it was breakable crust and I had a very bad fall. My foot went around two or three times and my leg was very badly broken in fourteen places. Both guides had me on a sledge in no time and I was carted off to hospital in Grindlewald where they tied up the broken bits with wire. It was a wonderful job with four double wires holding my whole leg together.

When I returned home, my mother-in-law said that I had to go to the top man, which was actually very good advice. She sent me to see Sir Reginald Watson-Jones, the Queen's orthopaedic surgeon. He was a dark haired, very sinister looking man who said to me, that I couldn't come back too often with a broken plaster. Whatever you do, he said, don't look after that leg. Bash it about, do what you like with it, and if you bust the plaster, that's splendid.

So I did everything in it. I mowed the lawn in it. I had a wheelchair tied behind the lawnmower. I drove my car. I was able to work all the pedals with one foot although God knows what the police would have said had I been caught. The advice was very good for it kept all the muscles going, as I had to be in plaster for a long time until he eventually chopped out the wires.

He was going to cost a lot but as I was insured, and working at Lloyds at the time, the whole thing was a grand Harley Street racket. On one occasion, I had a two o'clock appointment with him, but he was late. I had something else I wanted to do, so I gave him a bollocking. I said: 'now look here you've bloody well kept me waiting and I'm paying you a lot of money for this.' He hit the roof. He went absolutely berserk. He had obviously had a very good lunch with a dram or three, so I stormed out. A little bit later when he had sobered up, I went back to him and said I thought he should listen to me. I said I thought he had a huge income and it would be very much more sensible for him if I paid him in whisky, because I had noticed that he liked it, and that would be the best thing all round. He fairly quickly agreed and after that we were firm friends. But he was angry at being given a bollocking by this young whippersnapper.

***

Addie Prior, was in the Olympic Ski team with Sheena and Vora and subsequently married General Sir Digby Raeburn. She is quite a short lady, but very powerful physically and an excellent skier. They were all doing wind tunnel tests at Farnborough before the 1952 Olympics, trying to work out what sort of clothes to wear and what sort of position to get into to reduce drag. There was a silver model of an aeroplane mounted on to a ring of about twelve inches diameter, sitting on another ring below it of the same size. The bottom ring was perforated with a series of holes for compressed air to carry the top ring, without friction, so it was possible to turn the whole contraption with one's little finger when the air was turned on. It was being demonstrated by a chap who suggested that I should try the weight of the aeroplane. I found it really heavy and could only just lift it with two hands. I turned round to Addie who was watching, and offered it to her so that she could feel the weight. Addie took one hand to it and lifted it up just like that! She was incredibly strong. But she has hot hands, rather like Vora, but only more so with the power of healing in her hands.

I think these arduous things are nothing to do with being male or female, but entirely to do with excellence. A woman can do exactly the same thing as a man and in many ways, a woman has better resistance - in endurance terms - than a man. In wartime concentration camps for instance, very often it was the women who were better at surviving than the men. I believe that if you want a very efficient military unit, which our outfit most certainly was, the training was designed for excellence and one's own capacity, and it actually requires huge modesty that comes entirely from within. A man should find out as early as possible where his limits are - and then of course, he must exceed them...

The feminine body though should not really be mucked about in the same way, although today some do extreme climbs and other extreme sports, which are often incredible feats of athletic performance. But I also do think though that a woman is usually much better than a man at looking after a young family. If you want to have a family that is bought up with the best values for life, then there must be a very important role for the mother to be in the home in those early days. Sheena for example, was an absolutely superb mother. She delivered love and affection in spades, provided stability (despite my own antics) and made sure that she built up each of our children's confidence to the maximum extent possible. I as a man could never have achieved those things in that way.

CHAPTER THIRTEEN

Reflections

Well, that is a brief summary of my life so far. It has been fun and a great deal longer than I had any right to expect or hope for. I don't think I have very much to show for it all, except some absolutely fantastic children, grandchildren and even three great grandchildren, who all look good and without a bad egg amongst the lot.

I think divorce was a mistake and achieved precisely nothing, except that I suppose it enabled me to do exactly what I had wanted to do for some time and for Sheena to continue to live a life at Logie Farm.

I have minded about our Skye heritage for it really is unique. We are related to such a wide variety of society here. I do very much hope that this fascinating interest will continue. It is a rich tapestry that could not easily be matched I believe, and so full of wonderful people.

I also believe firmly that such a beautiful place will prosper in tomorrow's world. As technology's grip strengthens on our children, so the power and value of the countryside increases. The healthy mind and spirit the countryside imbues means that enterprise and opportunities must abound. The crazy rush to follow others is overwhelming the cities and urban life.

It is true that I have probably always attempted to do what I have been told not to do, not so much for devilry, but in the belief that behaving like sheep is not a good idea and it's not in my nature. I do not admire the philosophy of waiting for dead men's shoes to prevail, as it appears to me is the practice of many conventions.

I do love the concept of adventure. It is exciting to discover something or somewhere that one does not know about. Danger is a bit like spreading Marmite on toast to tickle up the senses, and sailing, skiing, flying and improvising all do just that. I suppose laughter forms the basis of my thinking, which Skye epitomises so well. The humour of what is not said is such fun here and I have grown to love that aspect of life.

All my growing up years in Skye now seem to have been one long adventure, with the war looming and then reality. The Scots Guards, the anti-climax of trying to be respectable, followed by Rhodesia and all that involved - which really felt like opening a new book; all those smells and excitement were a tonic to my senses, crushed when Philippa married Sandy.

I think the next period of attempting to follow what my parents seemed to expect of me was unreal, for I did not fit into the world of conventional business. I remember being deeply embarrassed when expected to get my friends to do their insurance through me and earn commission in the process.

All my life I have been fascinated by Bentleys. Grandfather Hilleary started it, my father continued the tradition, ending with the 8 litre GN1896. A wonderful car that caused W.O. Bentley to hand over to Rolls Royce because the 8 Litre Bentley was threatening to upstage the Rolls Royce Phantom. It did eight miles to a gallon of petrol and we once drove the 50 miles from Frankfurt to Heidleburg on the new Autobahn in half an hour, and really she was just ticking over. My father had a Speed Six before that, but I remember that he did not like the steering.

Later I had a 1923 Three Litre Bentley SD 7146 which was the 125th car built by WO Bentley. I sold it for £300 in about 1950. It now belongs to Paul Cooper who allowed me to drive Duncan and Sophie away from their wedding in it. It was then worth £70,000 and is probably worth £300,000 today. I followed that with a 4 ½ Litre Bentley HPA 246 in which Sheena and I drove south to announce our engagement in 1951, the time the engine exploded at around 100 mph.

As a final gesture, as a sort of 90th birthday present to myself, I have bought a 1997 Bentley Turbo R, P40 TSE, which is very beautiful and comfortable, although does not sound like the old "little bugger, big bugger" of WO's days; but she is fun to drive and I love the familiar flying "B" on the bonnet.

***

When I discovered the SAS was to be wound up after the war I took the opportunity to help prevent its disbandment and in the process found a niche that fitted exactly with my whole attitude and character. It epitomised all the qualities I admire most and aspire to emulate, although I have to admit to having seriously slowed down in recent years, yet the principles remain.

The sea has always drawn me to learn about its extent, its threats and its power. I first felt respect for its dangers when falling off the wrong side of a bridge over a river for a challenge when I was about six years old and somehow just had to swim without water wings for the first time. Fishing became an excitement when up to 100 haddock could be caught on hand lines locally, and then sailing started to take over.

I had to pass a test in Trieste after the war before being allowed to take one of the Club boats out alone; and there was Gladeye, the 100 ft Brigade Yacht Club yacht. But I suppose I learned more from Jock McLeod and Tony Stevenson about where the rocks were and how to avoid them ......well mostly avoid them!

The seasons pass and with them the endless change of senses from the first snowdrops in February/March heralding new life, to warmer weather; and the Cuillins shaking off their cover to demonstrate a power and magic that tingles down one's spine. Summer is not long in passing, somehow losing any thoughts of sunny beaches with showers and the inevitable midge. Why does everybody come to Skye at that silly time, when the May/June time is so very much better?

Shooting, fishing, skiing, sailing, stalking, climbing, walking, exploring all opened new horizons that made life for me. I am so grateful for having had the opportunity to do all these things and hopefully, open doors for my descendants to follow.

Trips to Kenya, Jerusalem, North Africa, Australia, New Zealand, Afghanistan and South Africa have all added spice to the tale. But Skye, at the end of it all, is my very special home, so beautifully expressed by Sheriff Alexander Nicholson:

Jerusalem, Athens and Rome
I'd see them before I die,
But I'd rather not see any one of the three
Than be exiled forever from Skye.

APPENDIX

Family History

The Hilleary, Robertson and MacLeod Families on Skye

My paternal grandparents were Major Edward Langdale Hilleary OBE. TD. DL. (1872 - 1939) and Edith Robertson - one of seven children. Edith's father, John Robertson, was originally from Perthshire.

The Hillearys descend originally from the Gooch family, who can be traced back to the middle 1500's as prosperous traders in and around Yarmouth in Norfolk. There was a Bishop Gooch ancestor who was born in 1684 and a baronetcy was given to a Sir William Gooch in 1746, probably because he was the Lieutenant Governor of Virginia from 1727 to 1749.

The fourth Baronet, Sir Thomas Gooch W O of Benacre Hall in Suffolk (1745 - 1826) produced two illegitimate sons, Gustavus and Robert, around 1795 with the daughter of a yeoman farmer who we think was named Sarah Mount. It seems the Gooch was quite kind and thoughtful towards these offspring, as he clearly educated them both very well and seems to have set them up as solicitors. Gustavus Hilleary lived into his eighties and produced Fredric Hilleary. He was also a solicitor and pillar of the law, and was the Town Clerk of West Ham, in London. Frederic's son was my Grandfather Edward (Teddy) Hilleary (1872 - 1939). He had at least four brothers and three sisters and was born in Essex. The family home was Bleak House, Stratford.

Grandad (Teddy) Hilleary was a lovely man. Educated at Charterhouse and Trinity College, Cambridge, where he read law. He was admitted as a solicitor in 1897 and practised briefly in London in his father's firm in Fenchurch St. All of his brothers went to Cambridge, and four of them, George, Frederic, Leicester and Teddy, became solicitors and worked, at the beginning in Fenchurch St.

But Teddy had more entrepreneurial, and possibly rebellious, instincts. Together with his youngest brother, Roland - Uncle Ro - Teddy gave up the law and set up The White Heather Laundry in the late eighteen hundreds, which was based in Willesden, North West London. As a result of this 'shocking' decision, they were cut off without a penny by their father for going into 'trade'.

But they actually made a huge success of the business and were eventually granted several Royal Appointments for The White Heather Laundry, so they must have been doing the Queen's smalls pretty effectively.

They had sizeable premises and the laundry was delivered by uniformed drivers in very smart liveried white and purple vans. I do not know why they wanted to start a laundry, but I think they just saw a need for it as an entrepreneurial enterprise – and it certainly paid off.

Grandad and Uncle Ro seemed very respectable sort of people though. This ran right through Grandad's life for he was clearly a man with a presence. Not particularly imposing, but very kindly. I remember he had a bald head at the end of his life – which, as a small child, I was sometimes allowed to smack.

Great Grandad Fredric Hilleary

He first came to Skye in the late 1800s with a Cambridge University friend, Sir William Tarn, reputedly the greatest Latin scholar of his day. Bill Tarn used to visit Skye as he loved the Island, and he invited my grandfather to come along. On one of those trips, he met my grandmother, Edith Robertson of Greshornish, who was from a very old Skye family. Skye society was fairly limited at that time with pretty well all the main houses related, so it would not have taken long to meet everybody of significance.

Teddy and Edith married in 1900 and had three sons: my father Iain in 1902, and then Kenneth (known as Uncle Rocky) and Somerled (known as Uncle Goo).

They lived in London in the early part of their marriage. On one census their address is given as 2 Albert Place, Kensington, W11. The laundry was very prosperous at that time and the couple used to come to Skye often and as the laundry continued to prosper, they spent more time there. Although The White Heather laundry was based in London, it also did the washing for many of the big houses in Skye. It was all sent to London, in big wicker baskets.

After a time Grandad and Uncle Ro expanded. They took over the firm of dry cleaners, Davis & Co and started another laundry called The Bluebird.

My Grandfather Major E.L. Hilleary OBE. TD. DL.

In Skye, Teddy and Edith had The Lodge at Edinbane, which had been the shooting Lodge for the Greshornish Estate. Teddy had a pale blue 4 1/4 litre Bentley in the garage, now the Edinbane Pottery, and servants in the house. I think the house was bought from his brother-in-law, Uncle Kenneth of Greshornish.

Eventually, Grandad Hilleary spent most of his time in Skye, with occasional trips to London.

Grandad was a man of tremendous principle. He had joined the Lovat Scouts in the first Great War, where he served as DAA & QMG in the Dardenelles campaign. He was Adjutant to Colonel Kenny Macdonald DSO of Tote at one time, and his many medals from that period included one from Greece for bravery. He was also mentioned in dispatches three times.

He later became so embroiled in Skye life that he became a member of Inverness County Council for Skye, served as Finance Convenor, from which post he resigned on a point of principle. He chaired the Report for the Government on the "Economic Conditions of the Highlands and Islands, with suggestions for improvement" which became known as The Hilleary Report. This was the forerunner of the Highland Development Board, or HIE as it has now become.

Grandad died in a nursing home in Surrey in 1939 but is buried in Edinbane cemetery. He was widely loved in Skye for his generosity and integrity and his epitaph is movingly remembered on his gravestone.

The Robertsons and Robertson Macleods

Granny Hilleary, Edith Robertson, came from a very old Skye family, that can be traced back about seven hundred years, starting with the 'tack' of Gesto, which we can track back to Murdo MacLeod on Loch Bracadale in 1332.

A tack is what an estate used to be called before the days of land ownership, it was a parcel of land granted to a tacksman by the Clan Chief. The tacksman, an early sort of factor, was appointed by the Chief and was responsible for collecting the rent and dues.

In the early 1800s Captain Neil MacLeod lost the tack of Gesto after a legal battle with the Chief, Sir Norman MacLeod of MacLeod of Dunvegan over the boundary of the tack. They were related so they used to dine together in Edinburgh, and then battle it out in court in Edinburgh during the day.

Captain Neil won the case and but the following year he was kicked out of Gesto, for the Chief was probably annoyed at losing the case. Captain Neil spent the remainder of his life haunting the libraries of Edinburgh to look for ways to regain his lease.

One of Captain Neil's sons, Kenneth MacLeod (Coinneach Mhor in Gaelic), left Skye for India in the early 1800s, aged 15 (Mrs Macdonald of Waternish gave him a golden guinea to help him on his way). His nephew, Lachlan Macdonald of Tote joined him there with other Skye emigrants, where they planted indigo, from which they made substantial fortunes.

In 1830 Kenneth returned to Skye and bought the estates of Greshornish, Orbost, Edinbane and Skeabost, which latter estate he sold to his nephew Lachlan Macdonald.

Kenneth also built the Hospital in Edinbane and laid out the present township with the various trades which were needed for building the big houses. He turned two small cottages into his mansion, now Greshornish Hotel, and the original Tacksman's house became his stables. This building is now known as The Orde, which I converted back to its original form, or something near to that and lived in during the early 1990s.

Kenneth MacLeod was a huge man in every sense of the word. He never married but left all his estates to his nephew, Kenneth Robertson - then aged five years - on condition that he added the name of MacLeod to his name, thus becoming Kenneth Robertson-MacLeod.

Kenneth Robertson MacLeod was born in 1864 at Snizort, the son of John Robertson and Isabella Macdonald of Ord on the south end of Skye. Isabella Macdonald was the daughter of Anne MacLeod of Gesto and a granddaughter of Captain Neil MacLeod. John Robertson and Isabella had 13 children of whom Kenneth was the third son, and Edith (Granny Hilleary) was their seventh daughter.

Kenneth Robertson-MacLeod later married Harriet, the daughter of General Stevenson, a former governor of Guernsey. She was known as Aunt Harrie.

Aunt Harrie had had ambitions on the stage in her early days and was a wonderfully colourful figure, with a long string of amber beads round her neck. She ensured laughter galore at Greshornish. They had a son "little darling Kenneth", who died one year after his birth in 1913, and was buried at Dhubaig near Greshornish, in a glorious deserted spot beside the loch. There is a memorial for him and his parents there still.

A second son, Roddy Robertson-MacLeod, DSO, MC, left Eton just before the war in 1939, a short time before I got there. He joined the Territorial Cameron Highlanders and was captured at St.Valery-en-Caux in Northern France, with the Highland Division. According to a recent article in the Daily Mail about him, he and his comrades were made to march all the way to Poland, and spent the rest of the war in camps across Poland and Germany.

Roddy made several attempts to escape from the camps, one of which involved being exported with the rubbish. However, all his attempts failed and when he returned to Skye after the war, he was assigned to the Royal Guard at Balmoral. It is said that he taught the Queen and Princess Margaret Highland dancing. After this he studied zoology at Cambridge.

In 1950, he broke the unwritten rule and married a brother officer's wife, Daphne Underwood, and so had to leave the Camerons for the King's Own Scottish Borderers, with whom he went to Korea as a Company Commander. In 1951 they had run out of ammunition so charged the Chinese with broken beer bottles, for which he was awarded the DSO for his 'magnificent leadership'.

Roddy then left the Army and was given command of the Police Training College at Tulliallan, at Kincardine Bridge, near Stirling , where he once told me that it was "the only place where they still call me Sir!" Roddy died in 1989, aged 69.

His sister Sheila sadly never married. She was rather a diffident person who spent her life looking after her mother, Aunt Harrie. I think she rather fancied my father but nothing ever came of that. She used to sculpt in a studio that she had in the Greshornish stables, (later to become The Orde).

The MacLeods

Rubie MacLeod, my mother.

My mother was Rubie MacLeod. Her parents were Duncan MacLeod CBE, of Skeabost, and Ishbel MacNeil. Grandad (Duncan) MacLeod, had been born in a very small thatched croft house at Breakish in the south end of Skye, one of the six children of Beatha Mackinnon of Strath and Donald MacLeod. The family had been crofters there for many generations that we can trace back to the late 1600s, but Grandad had left Skye and made more than one fortune having become a significant

With my mother

whisky magnate, before returning to Skye, to improve all of his family's situation.

Granny (Ishbel) MacLeod was born on a farm called The Cnoc (pronounced Cronk) on the Isle of Arran - she was of farming stock, rather than crofting I think.

They had six children and my mother Rubie was the eldest.

Aunt Mairi, Rubie's sister, married Julian Day, of the bankers Dawnay Day & Co. and had one daughter, Lavinia, who became Philip Rosenthal's fifth wife, and then had four children with him.

Then came Uncle Angus, who married Jean Carr, an Australian, in 1933. He was a tremendous character and very generous, but died very early as he hit the bottle too hard. They had one daughter, Catriona, who married Philip Wroughton, of Woolley Park, Wantage, later Sir Philip, KCB, Chairman of Bowrings and Lord Lieutenant of Berkshire.

Uncle Alan MacLeod, married Joan de Knoop and had three sons, twins Duncan and Jersey, and Iain. Uncle Alan was a Captain in the Territorial Cameron Highlanders, but was killed in Sicily in 1943. Duncan, his son, married Joanna Bibby, became Senior Partner of Ernst & Young

Great Granny 'Beatha' Mackinnon of Strath

Great Grandfather Angus and Beatha and their family.
With Duncan MacLeod on the right.

in Glasgow, was a Director of the Bank of Scotland and a number of other establishments and was awarded a CBE. Duncan had polio at Eton. I went to see him in his iron lung, and he couldn't move a muscle. He could move an eyelid, and that's about all he could do. He couldn't speak, it was absolutely terrible. It was just pure guts that pulled him through, really. He was so badly affected by the polio that he couldn't join the army.

His twin brother Jersey, who had been in the Cameron Highlanders, married Dauvergne Walker, but sadly died from injuries caused by two bad car crashes. The first happened on a German autobahn. A lorry came out in front of him and he drove underneath it. It was a horrible crash and he badly cracked his skull. He was invalided out of the army but recovered more or less. He took to the road again and soon had another crash, this time he was with Mike Hawthorn, a racing driver. I don't know why he was driving with him, but he was. Anyway, he cracked his skull again and that really finished him. He didn't die immediately but he did eventually.

In the meantime, between leaving the army after the first crash and before the second crash, Jersey ran Skeabost as a hotel. He went to learn about hotel management with Brian Franks who ran the Hyde Park Hotel and had commanded 21 SAS at the end of the war. So he got some quite serious training and my grandfather, Duncan MacLeod, had bought several hotels when he was on the up, one of which was the Royal Hotel in Portree which the family still have. Jersey was gentle and much loved by everyone but was not very demanding and rather quiet after the crash.

When Jersey died, Skeabost was sold. The people who bought it were called Stewart - a very nice family with strong Skye connections. They ran the hotel well and I think did quite well out of it. It had a very nice atmosphere, much as I remember it as a boy. When you go in the wood it smells just as it always did.

Duncan eventually sold the estate back to Johnny Macdonald of Tote, whose father Colonel Kenny had originally sold it to Grandad, following the calling in of the Bond on The Gesto Hospital, which had bust him. So it has gone full circle.

The youngest of Duncan and Ishbel's six children were twins, Uncle Jack (known as Jacko MacLeod), and Aunt Catriona MacLeod (known as Tushki). Uncle Jack was very good looking and occasionally rather cocky, I thought. He married Theodora Wills, who was very rich, before the war and they had twins, David and Carole, at Redcastle which they had rented. He did not meet the twins until the war ended. After the war Jack and Theo had three more children, Jocelyn, Martin and Mary Rose (known as Kipper).

Aunt Theo was a lovely generous person who had joined the Women's Auxiliary Air Force, ATA, during the war and used to ferry Spitfires and Hurricanes from the factories to the bases, so she was a real action girl.

Uncle Jack was captured at St.Valery and then spent the whole war in prison. On release he stood for Parliament and became the MP for Ross and Cromarty for 25 years, after which he was knighted and then lost his seat. He wasn't more than about ten years older than me, being the youngest of my mother's family and I was the eldest grandson, so he used to try and come the uncle with me a bit; but I wasn't having any of that so we crossed a sword or two.

David MacLeod, Jack and Theo's eldest son, died in 2009 and his twin sister Carole a few months later, in Kenya. She had married Peter Barclay, an Irish Guardsman who farms in big way but I think it is quite difficult now. He used to look after Kenyatta's farms, and I think is quite an important figure in the agriculture world. He drives his own aeroplane and is a lovely man. He fell off his horse playing polo which damaged his head a bit. Carole and Peter had a daughter, Karen, who married Jamie, son of Roddy Robertson MacLeod of Greshornish. They are not related to each other, but are both cousins of ours. Jamie is a tall splendid man who used to run Operation Raleigh.

Aunt Catriona MacLeod, or Tushki as we all knew her, was very beautiful. When she was young, Grandad MacLeod, took her to America on the Queen Mary. On the way out Percy Melville, an American playboy, tried to get into bed with her. She reportedly said - 'No, no, not unless we're married'. So they trotted along to the bridge and got the Captain to marry them. When Grandad discovered, he was absolutely furious and so tied up the money she was to have in a very tight trust. That marriage lasted about a fortnight and caused quite a scandal in the family, but then she found Joseph Herman, a Polish artist who became a very well known Royal Academician. I remember he wore a bootlace around his neck when he came to meet everyone at Skeabost for the first time and was a bit like a fish out of water.

***

I don't think Granny Hilleary (Edith) approved of my mother, Rubie, at all. New money was probably the view. They were a bit stuffy and Victorian like that.

My Father and Mother divorced after the War, in about 1945, very stupidly I thought. I think my parents' divorce came about as a result of a series of complicated things. They weren't together during the war and they drifted apart. My mother was very good looking and a lot of fun. She was very good company and had a lot of admirers who paid attention to her.

One was a man called Peter Spanoghe, who was a beak at Eton, with a limp because he'd had polio. He had a very beautiful wife. Then there was a fellow called Frank Giles who was an editor of The Sunday Times for a while. I didn't like him at all.

I was granted compassionate leave from the Scots Guards in Trieste to try to prevent my parents' divorce, unsuccessfully, but not before knocking Wilfrid de Knoop, Aunt Joan's brother who was in the Coldstream Guards, down the stairs when he announced that he was going to marry my mother.

I never did accept him, although they were clearly very happy together. My mother would not go back to live in Skye, as my father determined to do, for she wanted a broader kind of life I think. My Mother and Wilfrid, who was a Partner in Rowe & Pitman, and pretty thick I believe, rented a beautiful home at New Hall, Thorpe le Soken in Essex.

When he eventually retired, they went to live in what my Mother called "the Algrave". They built a lovely house, designed by Sir Basil Spence, the architect who had designed the new Coventry Cathedral and was quite a friend of theirs. It was up in the hills above Monchique, just a little bit too high because the mists often used to cover the hill down to just below their house. They had been sold the plot by a crooked old Gunner Brigadier who fancied my mother and was a ghastly snob.

Whenever I used to visit them, which I had to do much more frequently after Wilfred died, I used to always stop and try to buy the old Cadillac Fire Engine in Monchique. It was a classic, with lovely old brasses and I understood that if I could provide the "Bomberos" as they crew were called, with a more modem version, I could get the old one. I had visions of driving the splendid old character up through France to include a trip up the Champs Elysees with the hose going and the bell ringing.

However, my Portuguese was not really up to the job and so when I put the proposition to them one day, I discovered that I had been barking up the wrong tree and the deal was off.

My father repaired to live at Tayinloan after my parents' divorce. He then bought Beaton's Garage in Portree, now MacRae's, for that was the bus business for the island. He started a building business with a man called Walker, at what became Macdonald Bros & Co, and then he bought the Dunvegan Hotel. It did not have a licence and so I went with my father to the Licensing Court in Inverness, to hear the application.

The Minister in Dunvegan at that time was the Reverend Colquhoun, a strong "wee free", and of course violently opposed to the demon drink. When he was invited to state his objection to my father's application, he trotted out a long list of all the inhabitants of Dunvegan written out carefully in his own hand. Somewhat naturally, the licence was granted and poor old Colquhoun returned to Dunvegan, defeated.

I don't believe that I ever saw my father with dirty hands, for he seemed always to have somebody to do whatever had to be done. The result was of course, that his Skye enterprises, wholly splendid and well

My father Iain Hilleary CBE.

intentioned, did not work, and such money as he had began to dwindle. I think Skye should have been a gold mine. In fact, his whole Skye operation should have been a great success. But it really wasn't. He sold the buses. The building company folded up. Then he sold the hotel. This probably coincided with a certain amount of local works, which he did a lot of. Eventually that was his full-time thing. He became a full-time public servant... for all the right reasons. It was unpaid, but the expenses he got just about kept him afloat, although he did run himself into a bit of debt. He had some trust funds that he couldn't touch - he couldn't get the capital.

After quite a long period as a bachelor, my father married an elegant London-based lady called Rose Congreve who did have some money and they set about changing Tayinloan into a much more sophisticated establishment.

Rose didn't last for more than ten years. She was born Thorburn, then married a Congreve, of Irish extraction. That marriage failed but she had a daughter by him called Audrey, who married John Hanmer, who became a baronet - their son, Edward, is my godson. Audrey was at school with Sheena, my former wife.

Rose Congreve was really more interested in Chelsea than in Skye. She wrote novels, but I think the rain got her down. She turned Tayinloan inside out and back to front and painted it pink which was rather startling at the time, but actually rather nice. But it wasn't exactly what Skye had been used to. But she had some nice furniture, and I think, some money, which helped my father quite a lot, because I think he needed a rich wife to maintain the lifestyle.

It was all splendid for a bit. Then they bought a grocer's business in Hampstead, the purpose of which I think, was to go to Fortnum and Masons and buy stuff at a discount, which they then ended up eating. I think it was a cover story for a good larder. I don't think it made any profit, because all the profits were being shunted off to the house.

So my father spent a bit of time in London during the Rose era. He was a member of Brooks's Club in St James. His luggage was leather with nice polished brass. And he was immaculately turned out. He fitted into the scenery quite well as the Highland gentleman who came to London and went to the London club and sat drinking port and smoking cigars. He did put a good bit of weight on, but he never got fat.

Rose didn't really have any friends on Skye and I think got increasingly fed up with it. She had two big poodles. We took them out in the boat once and one of them got its ear caught in the propeller shaft which, very distressingly, tore its ear off. They were quite sporting dogs, although not the sort everyone was used to. But the fun started getting a bit thin. The Hampstead shop didn't really make any money, and my father rather enjoyed going around trying to find expensive things. The Minch Shipping and Trading Company was the cover story for some sort of enterprise, and he bought a fish shop in St James, off Jermyn Street. About that time the marriage to Rose failed.

There followed another period of some financial worry until he met an old friend from the early days, who had also had an unhappy married life, Joey Chrystal. This was a very happy and fortunate encounter that should have been the answer for them both, but fate was to intervene when Joey choked on a bit of meat while they were dining together.

By the time she reached hospital she had been dead for too long. They revived her but she was brain dead and remained so for more than a year with my father grieving at her bedside, convinced that she would awake and become the perfect wife once more.

It was a tragic end really for them both. My Father continued alone for a few years, but he never recovered his "joie de vivre". He died in Raigmore hospital of a heart attack. His epitaph should have included reference to his Public Service for Skye for which he was to get a CBE. He had served on The Council of Tribunals, was a Deputy Sheriff Substitute, and had been responsible for the upgrading of all the Highland Roads as Convenor of the Roads Committee on the old Inverness County Council. In fact, all these good roads, which we've now got on the island, are really due to him. The new road, which runs from Inverailort around to Loch Sunart, he built. He was also chairman of the Mallaig Harbour Authority.

As a public figure, my father was something of a legend in Skye I think, much respected and indeed loved by many. His life was not really a happy one although there had been very many tremendously happy interludes. Perhaps his problem was that he never did have to properly earn his living.

After he died, my father left me the Edinbane estate, which he'd bought for a thousand pounds, which I bought out from his estate for two thousand pounds. So his finances were dead wobbly.

***

My father's two brothers, Kenneth and Somerled, followed my Grandfather into the White Heather laundry.

Uncle Kenneth, was known as "Rocky" and Uncle Somerled, was known as "Goo" (because that is what he was reputed to have said as a baby!).

Rocky was an impossible man: he knew the answer to everything, and probably the best thing he ever did was to sack me from the White Heather Laundry.

He had been a very good athlete, playing football for the Corinthian Casuals and possibly even for England. But he bust his leg very badly and was quite badly incapacitated after that. He loved the sea and his launch. He married Aunt Gay, who was the Hon Grace Best. Her father was Lord Wynford, her mother was the daughter of Lord Napier. Lord Napier did the Napier Commission, which was responsible for the fixing of rents on crofting estates. There is a statue to him outside the Albert Hall at Queen's Gate.

Lord Napier expanded and improved the house at Lyndale near Edinbane.

Rocky and Gay had three daughters. Shena, Wendy and Jilly. Shena married Harry Cornell, a naval officer, and had a daughter, Nicky who married Richard Staveley and had a daughter Miranda.

Wendy married Ian Hedderwick who was planning to farm Lyndale. However, Uncle Rocky decided, just before he died of cancer in 1970, that they couldn't make a go of it, so he shipped Ian and Wendy off to Australia, telling them he was going to sell Lyndale, which was a terrible thing to do. But he thought he knew the answer to everything and he thought they were never going to prosper. So he sold Lyndale for nothing to an idiot man who let it go to ruin. It was later sold to Marcus and Linda Ridsdill-Smith, who live there still.

Jilly married Duncan Bengough, an ex-Black Watch officer who became a prep-school master.

Goo was huge, about six foot six. He couldn't have been far short of twenty stone, and we couldn't get him into the grave when we buried him because they had not made the hole big enough. He was supposed to run the Bluebird laundry, an offshoot of the White Heather, but he did not appear there until about 11 am each morning when he would arrive in his rubber soled brown shoes from Fortnum & Mason, to read The Times and then have lunch.

A quick look at the mail and a nap, then round to his Club for tea turned his day into a riot before returning home to his very "Scotch" wife, Mickey. They sadly had no children so his not inconsiderable fortune went to an au pair girl on his demise. Mickey used to say "poor Goo" in her kind way, for she doted on him in spite of his quite incredible indolence.

The Highlander's Prayer

Oh that the peats would cut themselves
And the fish jump out on the shore
And I would sit by the fireside
And sleep forever more

(By Mairi MacNab for my 90th birthday)
An Ode to Ruaraidh E.M.R.Hilleary
8/2/2016

The Rovers Return

Your dream of a windfarm came to fruition,
One of your many exciting ambitions
You've done us all proud as many can see
As the Edinbane tenants are happy with glee.

Normally by ninety the body slows down
But not for you Ruaraidh—your spirit won't drown
Due to the Oysters and Whisky galore
We've cancelled the Care Plan for you in Budhmor.

An exciting new asset you purchased last year
And heads keep on turning to gaze at your rear.
The classic old Bentley is of course what I mean
A bird pulling motor to keep them all keen.

A magnet to women you always have been
Even blown up dolls—not many have seen!
They flock like the Grouse to be by your side
As you wait for the salmon on the oncoming tide.

When out in the Bentley and fuels running low
You head for the forecourt with sporran in tow
Donnie & John rub their hands with delight
At seeing this old classic—a wonderful sight.

In 10 year's time your landmark will be
A century of life we all hope to see
Good Luck, Health & Happiness and a 4 leaf Clover
So keep the kilt swinging you wild Highland Rover.

About the Author

Adventurer, sailor, skier, entrepreneur and former member of the Territorial SAS, Ruaraidh Hilleary has led an exciting life. His memoirs cover his idyllic childhood in the Isle of Skye in the 1930s, schooldays at Eton during the war, followed by postings with the Scots Guards that included Trieste and the bombed ruins of Cologne. He has canoed the Zambezi river, nearly fallen into a crevasse in the Swiss Alps and experienced the Cresta Run and the bobsleigh in St Moritz, without brakes.

His professional life has been equally intrepid. Ruaraidh sold cutlery in Zimbabwe, insurance in London, smoked salmon in Paris, cashmere in Spain and even Highland Wine in Scotland. He also owned and ran a caravan park near Lossiemouth in the 1970s and has helped develop a fish farm with the Jethro Tull rock star Ian Anderson and a wind farm in partnership with Amec, both on Skye, where he now lives.

Ruaraidh's book documents a life filled with challenges, risks, much laughter and some sadness. Now a well-known, much-loved Skye figure, a father, grandfather and great-grandfather, 'Whatever you are doing, don't' contains fascinating insights into Scotland's recent history, as well as reflections on 90 years of a life, in which every minute was lived to the full.

"So I did it anyway"

16260560R00112

Printed in Poland
by Amazon Fulfillment
Poland Sp. z o.o., Wrocław